Postscripts

CW00495919

O. Henry

Alpha Editions

This edition published in 2024

ISBN 9789361475801

Design and Setting By

Alpha Editions
www.alphaedis.com

Email - info@alphaedis.com

Contents

Foreword

It is probable that with the presentation of these, among the earliest of the writings of William Sidney Porter (O. Henry), there is nothing left to be added to the total of his work, and that they will close, as they in a large measure opened the career of America's greatest short story writer.

Aside from the intrinsic merit in the newspaper writings of O. Henry which are here given, they have the additional fascination of disclosing to all who have read and know O. Henry from his maturer work the budding of his genius, the first outcroppings of that style, that vivid drawing of character, that keen sense of humor, and that wondrous understanding of human nature which afterward marked him as one of the world's geniuses. It is as though one might go back and watch with eyes that have seen its fullest development and matured beauty, the forming and unfolding of a rose; as though one who has listened to the plaudits of centuries might go back four hundred years and see and study Raphael as he began to wield the brush which subsequently wrought such wonderful magic.

Having a high appreciation of the genius of O. Henry, the compiler took occasion while spending a year in Austin, Texas, where O. Henry had lived, to ask his friends and neighbors about him. Among them was Mr. Ed McLean, secretary to the railroad commission, a personal friend of O. Henry's, who told her about the column O. Henry had conducted on the Houston *Post.* He thought O. Henry must have worked for the *Post* some time in the latter part of 1896 to the fall of 1897.

A visit to the Houston *Post* office and a search through the files of that period were without results. But a call on Mr. A. E. Clarkson, who was with the *Post* then and who is now business manager of the *Post,* was more successful. Mr. Clarkson looked up the old records in the business office, showing when O. Henry received pay checks, which served as a guide to pages of a year earlier, where the altogether distinctive touch of O. Henry proved that the goal was reached. Here was found the same discernment, the same insight, the same humor, the same style which runs through all his work like a marked thread interwoven into a rare fabric. In many of the brief paragraphs and short stories were found the idioplasm which in the rich soil of his fuller experience grew into some of the masterpieces of his later life.

Thus in the files of the Houston *Post* of the period between October 18, 1895, and June 22, 1896, were found the writings which make up this volume. It was characteristic of O. Henry's modesty that these were unsigned. They are published as they originally appeared in "Tales of the Town," "Postscripts and Pencillings," and "Some Postscripts," under which titles O. Henry wrote at different times during his association with the *Post.*

But the rediscovery of this work was not enough. To identify it as beyond question of doubt as that of O. Henry was imperative. To have offered these writings with less of precaution would have savored of literary vandalism, if not sacrilege. This identification has been made, and its sources are herewith given the reader as a part of the introduction of this volume.

Here is an account by Mr. R. M. Johnston, who formerly controlled the Houston *Post*, of how he gave O. Henry the job in which he was first to demonstrate his remarkable story-telling gifts:

> Houston, Texas, October 21, 1922.
>
> Miss Florence Stratton,
> Beaumont, Texas.
>
> My dear Miss Stratton:
>
> You asked me to write some incidents of O. Henry's connection with the Houston *Post* when I controlled that newspaper and I am glad to comply with your request.
>
> The first thing I ever heard of Mr. Porter, whose writing name was O. Henry, was when some one sent me a copy of the little publication, "The Rolling Stone," published in Austin. This was sent me by Mr. Ed McLean, Secretary of the Railroad Commission, a mutual friend of Mr. Porter and myself. Mr. McLean made the suggestion that Porter would be worth considering for a place as a writer on the *Post.* After reading *The Rolling Stone* I made an appointment through Mr. McLean with Mr. Porter, who was at that time an employe of one of the banks at Austin. Subsequently I met him and made a contract with him to join the *Post* editorial staff which he did in a short time. While on the paper his duties were somewhat of a varied nature. He had, however, a column on the editorial page daily filled with witticism, quaint little stories, etc. He also did some special assignment work in a very magnificent way.

One morning while sitting at my desk he came to my office in his usual quiet, dignified way and laid a piece of cardboard on my table with the remark, "I don't suppose you will want this, but I thought I would let you look at it," and he walked out. After he had gone, I picked up the cardboard and found it was an unusual cartoon. I was so struck with it that I took it to his room and remarked, "Porter, did you do this?" He looked up with a faint smile, and said "Yes." I said to him that I did not know that he was a cartoonist, and his reply was that he did that kind of work for his own amusement at odd times.

To make a long story short, we were in the midst of a very warm political campaign in Texas and during the campaign he drew some of the most magnificent cartoons that I have ever seen in print anywhere. They attracted attention, not only in Texas, but were copied freely throughout the United States.

Mr. Porter was a lovely character and one of the brightest men that I have ever come in contact with. He was modest, almost to the fault of self-effacement. His leaving the Houston *Post* was an irretrievable loss to the paper, but the means possibly of developing the greatest short story writer of this or any other age.

Very sincerely your friend,

(Signed) R. M. Johnston.

A letter from former Governor Hobby of Texas, who worked with O. Henry on the *Post* during the time that he was producing the column:

Office of
W. P. HOBBY
Houston,
Texas.

502 Carter Building,
Houston, Texas.
October 10, 1922.

Miss Florence Stratton,
Beaumont, Texas.

My dear Miss Stratton:

In the first years of my employment by the Houston *Post*, O. Henry, whose name was Sidney Porter, was a member of the *Post* staff. As is well known, Mr. Porter began his daily journalistic work as a special feature writer for the Houston *Post* and the human interest and literary attractiveness of his writings were a source of delight to Texas readers.

I enjoyed my acquaintance and association with Mr. Porter while a youth in the business office of the Houston *Post* and not only the stories that he would write, but those he would tell me, made a deep impression on my mind.

Mr. Porter's work was that of publishing a special feature column, "Some Postscripts and Pencillings" on the editorial page of the *Post* during 1895–96, and I think a reproduction of his daily writings in that column, which then were followed by the readers of the Texas newspaper readers of the nation.

Yours very truly,

(Signed) W. P. Hobby.

Mr. A. E. Clarkson, secretary-treasurer of the Houston *Post*, authenticates the O. Henry column from his personal knowledge.

Houston, Texas.
October 16, 1922.

Miss Florence Stratton,
2020 Harrison,
Beaumont, Texas.

My dear Miss Stratton:

In reply to your letter of October 15, I find that Mr. Porter, afterward known as O. Henry, was on the payroll of the Houston *Post* from October 1895 to June 1896.

During that time Mr. Porter wrote, and there was published from time to time in the columns of the *Post* various articles headed "Some Postscripts" and "Postscripts and Pencillings."

The writer was also connected with the *Post* during this period, being in the business office. He was personally acquainted with Mr. Porter and knows of his own knowledge that the articles headed as stated above were written by him.

Yours truly,

THE HOUSTON POST

(Signed) A. E. Clarkson,

Business Manager.

Neither the compilation, verification, nor publication of these newspaper writings of O. Henry would have been possible without the co-operation of Mr. Roy G. Watson, present proprietor and publisher of the Houston *Post*, whose consent for their publication has been generously given; and of Governor William P. Hobby, Colonel R. M. Johnston, and Mr. A. E. Clarkson, all associated with the *Post* during O. Henry's employment, and to these, whose attestation of authenticity of this work is herewith given, the compiler is grateful. The doing of this work has been a labor of love, and if the result is to add to the luster of O. Henry's name the writer shall have been repaid.

No pen is so facile as to add to or detract from the fame of William Sidney Porter. The flame of his genius has been extinguished, but what he wrought in a vast understanding of humanity will ever illuminate American literature.

Florence Stratton.

April, 1923.

O. Henry on the Houston *Post*

With respect to O. Henry's services, the Houston Post states as follows:

Between musty covers of the *Post* files from October, 1895, to July, 1896, are cross-sections of life drawn by a master artist; vignettes as perfect and as beautiful as the finest Amsterdam diamond. Only they are comparatively unknown because they have been overshadowed by larger and more brilliant creations of the same master hand.

Verses beautiful and appealing; description, touched by wonderful imagery; dialogue, the lines of which sparkle with wit and understanding of human frailties!

They make up O. Henry's "Tales of the Town," his "Postscripts and Pencillings," and his "Some Postscripts." Save for the publication for a brief space of *The Rolling Stone*, a rollicking sheet that was issued irregularly over the period of several months, they represent the sum total of O. Henry's newspaper writings.

All too brief to suit lovers of O. Henry's work, they nevertheless betray the writer's knack of getting at the heart and mind of his fellow beings. They show him as well acquainted with the newsdealer on the corner as with his favorite hotel clerk; as much at home in talking with a puncher from the Panhandle as in conversing with a drummer from St. Louis. Into them the master of the short story managed to crowd uncanny description, insight into human nature, and the highly dramatic.

O. Henry came to the *Post* at the invitation of its editor and his first column appeared in the *Post* on October 18th entitled "Tales of the Town." The caption soon changed to "Postscripts and Pencillings" and later still to "Some Postscripts."

Some days a column of seven-point! Others only half a column. Still others when "Some Postscripts" failed to appear at all.

But always, whatever the quantity, the quality of O. Henry's output remained at high level.

As in the later days in New York, O. Henry was exceedingly modest and shy. He "took a little getting acquainted with" according to tradition handed down. A quiet, unassuming chap, with eyes which seemingly saw little and yet took in everything, the new member of the staff soon acquired a reputation of being the best listener in town. In addition, he was a painstakingly accurate reporter and observer.

O. Henry came to the *Post* under his real name of Sidney Porter, but it was as "The Post Man" that he referred to himself in his writings. The pronoun "I" seldom appeared.

According to friends, O. Henry, or Sidney Porter, possessed the most valuable trick of the interviewer. When the telling of a story lagged momentarily, he would insert just the right question in just the right place. And this show of interest never failed to stimulate the teller to a fresh spurt.

Favorite haunts in Houston were the lobby of the old Hutchins House, the Grand Central Depot, and the street corners. He used to sit for hours in the hotel, his eyes playing over the faces of guests. Mayhap he was studying types, who knows? Certain, though, it is that hotel attaches grew to love the author of "Some Postscripts," and they frequently went out of their way to send him word of stories on the old hotel's ancient register.

At the Grand Central Depot—Grand Central then as now—"The Post Man" was loved by all who knew him. From station master to porter, from superintendent to telegraph operator, the writer of "Some Postscripts" got help and inspiration for many of his brilliant anecdotes and human interest stories.

Then, as later in New York, it was the man in the street who claimed his chief attention. Feted though he was by some who thought to patronize him, "The Post Man" refused to allow his head to be turned by admiration. He continued the even tenor of his way, writing the things which most appealed to him.

Abundant and spontaneous as was O. Henry's literary output, his jokes were never barbed. There is no record of anyone ever coming to the *Post* editorial room to "lick" the author of "Some Postscripts." Rather there came to him many picturesque figures of the Southwest, eager to make the acquaintance of the rising young "colyumist."

At a time when bicycles and bloomers were agitating the news writers of the country, O. Henry took delight in caricaturing the customs. His sketches of bloomered, career-seeking women and timid husbands are at once a delight and a revelation.

O. Henry's brilliant style, together with his never-flagging wit and his seemingly inexhaustible fund of anecdote quickly captured his contemporaries among Texas newspaper men. "The man, woman, or child," wrote an exchange in 1896, "who pens 'Some Postscripts' in the Houston *Post*, is a weird genius, and ought to be captured and put on exhibition."

It was soon after this that O. Henry was advised to go to New York, where his ability would command a higher remuneration. But after making all preparations to try his wings in the great metropolis, Fate intervened and O. Henry went instead to South America.

The last columns of O. Henry's brilliant paragraphs appeared in the *Post* of June 22, 1896.

Postscripts

The Sensitive Colonel Jay

The sun is shining brightly, and the birds are singing merrily in the trees! All nature wears an aspect of peace and harmony. On the porch of a little hotel in a neighboring county a stranger is sitting on a bench waiting for the train, quietly smoking his pipe.

Presently a tall man wearing boots and a slouch hat, steps to the door of the hotel from the inside with a six-shooter in his hand and fires. The man on the bench rolls over with a loud yell as the bullet grazes his ear. He springs to his feet in amazement and wrath and shouts:

"What are you shooting at me for?"

The tall man advances with his slouch hat in his hand, bows and says: "Beg pardon, sah. I am Colonel Jay, sah, and I understood you to insult me, sah, but I see I was mistaken. Am very glad I did not kill you, sah."

"I insult you—how?" inquires the stranger. "I never said a word."

"You tapped on the bench, sah, as much as to say you was a woodpeckah, sah, and I belong to the other faction. I see now that you was only knockin' the ashes from you' pipe, sah. I ask yo' pahdon, and that you will come in and have a drink with me, sah, to show that you do not harbor any ill feeling after a gentleman apologizes to you, sah."

A Matter of Loyalty

Two men were talking at the Grand Central depot yesterday, and one of them was telling about a difficulty he had recently been engaged in.

"He said I was the biggest liar ever heard in Texas," said the man, "and I jumped on him and blacked both his eyes in about a minute."

"That's right," said the other man, "a man ought to resent an imputation of that sort right away."

"It wasn't exactly that," said the first speaker, "but Tom Achiltree is a second cousin of mine, and I won't stand by and hear any man belittle him."

Taking No Chances

"Let's see," said the genial manager as he looked over the atlas. "Here's a town one might strike on our way back. Antananarivo, the capital of Madagascar, is a city of 100,000 inhabitants."

"That sounds promising," said Mark Twain, running his hands through his busy curls, "read some more about it."

"The people of Madagascar," continued the genial manager, reading from his book, "are not a savage race and few of the tribes could be classed as barbarian people. There are many native orators among them, and their language abounds in figures, metaphors, and parables, and ample evidence is given of the mental ability of the inhabitants."

"Sounds like it might be all right," said the humorist, "read some more."

"Madagascar is the home," read the manager, "of an enormous bird called the epyornis, that lays an egg 15½ by 9½ in. in size, weighing from ten to twelve pounds. These eggs—"

"Never mind reading any more," said Mark Twain. "We will not go to Madagascar."

The Other Side of It

There is an item going the rounds of the press relative to the well-known curiosity of woman. It states that if a man brings a newspaper home out of which a piece has been clipped his wife will never rest until she has procured another paper to see what it was that had been cut out.

A Houston man was quite impressed with the idea, so he resolved to make the experiment. One night last week he cut out of the day's paper a little two-inch catarrh cure advertisement, and left the mutilated paper on the table where his wife would be sure to read it.

He picked up a book and pretended to be interested, while he watched her glance over the paper. When she struck the place where the piece had been cut, she frowned and seemed to be thinking very seriously.

However, she did not say anything about it and the man was in doubt as to whether her curiosity had been aroused or not.

The next day when he came home to dinner she met him at the door with flashing eyes and an ominous look about her jaw.

"You miserable, deceitful wretch!" she cried. "After living all these years with you to find that you have been basely deceiving me and leading a double life, and bringing shame and sorrow upon your innocent family! I always thought you were a villain and a reprobate, and now I have positive proof of the fact."

"Wh—wha—what do you mean, Maria?" he gasped. "I haven't been doing anything."

"Of course you are ready to add lying to your catalogue of vices. Since you pretend not to understand me—look at this."

She held up to his gaze a complete paper of the issue of the day before.

"You thought to hide your actions from me by cutting out part of the paper, but I was too sharp for you."

"Why that was just a little joke, Maria. I didn't think you would take it seriously. I—"

"Do you call that a joke, you shameless wretch?" she cried, spreading the paper before him.

The man looked and read in dismay. In cutting out the catarrh advertisement he had never thought to see what was on the other side of it, and this was the item that appeared, to one reading the other side of the page, to have been clipped:

> A gentleman about town, who stands well in business circles, had a high old time last night in a certain restaurant where he entertained at supper a couple of chorus ladies belonging to the comic opera company now in the city. Loud talking and breaking of dishes attracted some attention, but the matter was smoothed over, owing to the prominence of the gentleman referred to.

"You call that a joke, do you, you old reptile," shrieked the excited lady. "I'm going home to mamma this evening and I'm going to stay there. Thought you'd fool me by cutting it out, did you? You sneaking, dissipated old snake you! I've got my trunk nicely packed and I'm going straight home—don't you come near me!"

"Maria," gasped the bewildered man. "I swear I—"

"Don't add perjury to your crimes, sir!"

The man tried unsuccessfully to speak three or four times, and then grabbed his hat and ran downtown. Fifteen minutes later he came back bringing two new silk dress patterns, four pounds of caramels, and his bookkeeper and three clerks to prove that he was hard at work in the store on the night in question.

The affair was finally settled satisfactorily, but there is one Houston man who has no further curiosity about woman's curiosity.

Journalistically Impossible

"Did you report that suicide as I told you to do last night?" asked the editor of the new reporter, a graduate of a school of journalism.

"I saw the corpse, sir, but found it impossible to write a description of the affair."

"Why?"

"How in the world was I to state that the man's throat was cut from ear to ear when he had only one ear?"

The Power of Reputation

One night last week in San Antonio a tall, solemn-looking man, wearing a silk hat, walked into a hotel bar from the office, and stood by the stove where a group of men were sitting smoking and talking. A fat man, who noticed him go in, asked the hotel clerk who it was. The clerk told his name and the fat man followed the stranger into the barroom, casting at him glances of admiration and delight.

"Pretty cold night, gentlemen, for a warm country," said the man in the silk hat.

"Oh—ha—ha—ha—ha—ha!" yelled the fat man, bursting into a loud laugh. "That's pretty good."

The solemn man looked surprised and went on warming himself at the stove.

Presently one of the men sitting by the stove said:

"That old Turkey over in Europe doesn't seem to be making much noise now."

"No," said the solemn man, "it seems like the other nations are doing all the gobbling."

The fat man let out a yell and laid down and rolled over and over on the floor. "Gosh ding it," he howled, "that's the best thing I ever heard. Ah—ha—ha—ha—ha—ha! Come on, gentlemen, and have something on that."

The invitation seemed to all hands to be a sufficient apology for all his ill-timed merriment, and they ranged along the bar. While the drinks were being prepared, the fat man slipped along the line and whispered something in the ear of everyone, except the man with the silk hat. When he got through a broad smile spread over the faces of the crowd.

"Well, gentlemen, here's fun!" said the solemn man as he raised his glass.

The whole party, with one accord, started off into a perfect roar of laughter, spilling half their drinks on the bar and floor.

"Did you ever hear such a flow of wit?" said one.

"Chock full of fun, ain't he?"

"Same old fellow he used to be."

"Best thing that's been got off here in a year."

"Gentlemen," said the solemn man, "there seems to be a conspiracy among you to guy me. I like a joke myself, but I like to know what I'm being hurrahed about."

Three men lay down in the sawdust and screamed, and the rest fell in chairs and leaned against the bar in paroxysms of laughter. Then three or four of them almost fought for the honor of setting them up again. The solemn man was suspicious and watchful, but he drank every time anyone proposed to treat. Whenever he made a remark, the whole gang would yell with laughter until the tears ran from their eyes.

"Well," said the solemn man, after about twenty rounds had been paid for by the others, "the best of friends must part. I've got to get to my downy couch."

"Good!" yelled the fat man. "Ha—ha—ha—ha—ha! 'Downy couch' is good. Best thing I ever heard. You are as good, by Gad, as you ever were. Never heard such impromptu wit. Texas is proud of you, old boy."

"Good night, gentlemen," said the solemn man. "I've got to get up early in the morning and go to work."

"Hear that!" shouted the fat man. "Says he's got to work. Ha—ha—ha—ha—ha!"

The whole crowd gave a parting roar of laughter as the solemn man walked to the door. He stopped for a moment and said: "Had a very (hic) pleasant evening (hic) gents. Hope'll shee you (hic) 'n mornin'. Here'sh my card. Goo' night."

The fat man seized the card and shook the solemn man's hand. When he had gone, he glanced at the card, and his face took on a serious frown.

"Gentlemen," he said, "you all know who our friend is that we have been entertaining, don't you?"

"Of course; you said it was Alex Sweet, the 'Texas Siftings' man."

"So I understood," said the fat man. "The hotel clerk said it was Alex Sweet."

He handed them the card and skipped out the side door. The card read:

L. X. Wheat

Representing Kansas City

Smith and Jones Mo.

Wholesale Undertakers' Supplies

The crowd was out $32 on treats, and they armed themselves and are laying for the fat man. When a stranger attempts to be funny in San Antonio now, he has to produce proper credentials in writing before he can raise a smile.

The Distraction of Grief

The other day a Houston man died and left a young and charming widow to mourn his loss. Just before the funeral, the pastor came around to speak what words of comfort he could, and learn her wishes regarding the obsequies. He found her dressed in a becoming mourning costume, sitting with her chin in her hand, gazing with far-off eyes in an unfathomable sea of retrospection.

The pastor approached her gently, and said: "Pardon me for intruding upon your grief, but I wish to know whether you prefer to have a funeral sermon preached, or simply to have the service read."

The heartbroken widow scarcely divined his meaning, so deeply was she plunged in her sorrowful thoughts, but she caught some of his words, and answered brokenly:

"Oh, red, of course. Red harmonizes so well with black."

A Sporting Interest

It is a busy scene in the rear of one of Houston's greatest manufacturing establishments. A number of workmen are busy raising some heavy object by means of blocks and tackles. Somehow, a rope is worn in two by friction, and a derrick falls. There is a hurried scrambling out of the way, a loud jarring crash, a cloud of dust, and a man stretched out dead beneath the heavy timbers.

The others gather round and with herculean efforts drag the beams from across his mangled form. There is a hoarse murmur of pity from rough but kindly breasts, and the question runs around the group, "Who is to tell her?"

In a neat little cottage near the railroad, within their sight as they stand, a bright-eyed, brownhaired young woman is singing at her work, not knowing that death has snatched away her husband in the twinkling of an eye.

Singing happily at her work, while the hand that she had chosen to protect and comfort her through life lies stilled and fast turning to the coldness of the grave!

These rough men shrink like children from telling her. They dread to bear the news that will change her smiles to awful sorrow and lamentation.

"You go, Mike," three or four of them say at once. "'Tis more larnin' ye have than any av us, whatever, and ye'll be afther brakin' the news to her as aisy as ye can. Be off wid ye now, and shpake gently to Tim's poor lassie while we thry to get the corpse in shape."

Mike is a pleasant-faced man, young and stalwart, and with a last look at his unfortunate comrade he goes slowly down the street toward the cottage where the fair young wife—alas, now a widow—lives.

When he arrives, he does not hesitate. He is tenderhearted, but strong. He lifts the gate latch and walks firmly to the door. There is something in his face, before he speaks, that tells her the truth.

"What was it?" she asks, "spontaneous combustion or snakes?"

"Derrick fell," says Mike.

"Then I've lost my bet," she says. "I thought sure it would be whisky."

Life, messieurs, is full of disappointments.

Had a Use for It

A strong scent of onions and the kind of whisky advertised "for mechanical purposes" came through the keyhole, closely followed by an individual bearing a bulky manuscript under his arm about the size of a roll of wall paper.

The individual was of the description referred to by our English cousins as "one of the lower classes," and by Populist papers as "the bone and sinew of the country," and the scene of his invasion was the sanctum of a great Texas weekly newspaper.

The editor sat at his desk with his hands clenched in his scanty hair, gazing despairingly at a typewritten letter from the house where he bought his paper supply.

The individual drew a chair close to the editor and laid the heavy manuscript upon the desk, which creaked beneath its weight.

"I've worked nineteen hours upon it," he said, "but it's done at last."

"What is it?" asked the editor, "a lawn mower?"

"It is an answer, sir, to the President's message: a refutation of each and every one of his damnable doctrines, a complete and scathing review of every assertion and every false insidious theory that he has advanced."

"About how many—er—how many pounds do you think it contains?" said the editor thoughtfully.

"Five hundred and twenty-seven pages, sir, and—"

"Written in pencil on one side of the paper?" asked the editor, with a strange light shining in his eye.

"Yes, and it treats of—"

"You can leave it," said the editor, rising from his chair. "I have no doubt I can use it to advantage."

The individual, with a strong effort, collected his breath and departed, feeling that a fatal blow had been struck at those in high places.

Ten minutes later six india-rubber erasers had been purchased, and the entire office force were at work upon the manuscript.

The great weekly came out on time, but the editor gazed pensively at his last month's unreceipted paper bill and said:

"So far, so good; but I wonder what we will print on next week!"

The Old Landmark

He was old and feeble and his sands of life were nearly run out. He walked with faltering steps along one of the most fashionable avenues in the city of Houston. He had left the city twenty years ago, when it was little more than a thriving village, and now, weary of wandering through the world and filled with an unutterable longing to rest his eyes once more upon the scenes of his youth, he had come back to find a bustling modern city covering the site of his former home. He sought in vain for some familiar object, some old time sight that would recall memories of bygone days. All had changed. On the site where his father's cottage had stood, a stately mansion reared its walls; the vacant lot where he had played when a boy, was covered with modern buildings. Magnificent lawns stretched on either hand, running back to palatial dwellings. Not one of the sights of his boyhood days was left.

Suddenly, with a glad cry, he rushed forward with renewed vigor. He saw before him, untouched by the hand of man and unchanged by time, an old familiar object around which he had played when a child. He reached out his arms and ran toward it with a deep sigh of satisfaction.

Later on they found him asleep, with a peaceful smile on his face, lying on the old garbage pile in the middle of the street, the sole relic of his boyhood's recollections.

A Personal Insult

Young lady in Houston became engaged last summer to one of the famous shortstops of the Texas baseball league.

Last week he broke the engagement, and this is the reason why.

He had a birthday last Tuesday and she sent him a beautiful bound and illustrated edition of Coleridge's famous poem, "The Ancient Mariner."

The hero of the diamond opened the book with a puzzled look.

"What's dis bloomin' stuff about, anyways?" he said, and read:

> It is the Ancient Mariner
> And he stoppeth one of three—

The famous shortstop threw the book out the window, stuck out his chin and said:

"No Texas sis can gimme de umpire face like dat. I swipes nine daisy cutters outer ten dat comes in my garden, I do."

Toddlekins

Toddlekins climbed up the long, long stair;
Chubby and fat and round was he;
With rosy cheeks and curling hair,
Jolly and fair and gay was he.

Toddlekins knocked on the office door;
Within at a desk a stern man sat;
Wrote with a pen while a frown he wore,
When he heard on the door a rat-tat-tat.

Toddlekins cried, "Oh please let me in!
I've come to see you, the door is fast!"
Oh, voice so soft, it will surely win
The heart of the stern, cold man at last!

But he heeded not the pleading cry
Of Toddlekins out on the lonely stair;
And Toddlekins left with a sorrowful sigh,
Toddlekins round, and chubby and fair,

Oh, man so stem, when you stand and plead
At the door of your Father's house on high;

What if he, merciless, pay no heed;
Pitiless, turns from your helpless cry!

But the man wrote on with a stony stare;
He was an editor, poor and ill;
And Toddlekins, chubby and round and fair,
Was a butcher that brought a big meat bill.

Reconciliation

A One-Act Drama

Dramatis Personae—A Houston married couple.
Scene—Her boudoir.

He — And now, Viola, since we understand each other, let us never fall out again. Let us forget the bitter words that we have spoken one to another, and resolve to dwell always in love and affection. (*Places his arm around her waist.*)

She — Oh, Charles, you don't know how happy you make me! Of course we will never quarrel again. Life is too short to waste in petty bickerings and strife. Let us keep in the primrose path of love, and never stray from it any more. Oh, what bliss to think you love me and nothing can ever come between us! Just like the old days when we used to meet by the lilac hedge, isn't it? (*Lays her head on his shoulder.*)

He — Yes, and when I used to pull blossoms and twine them in your hair and call you Queen Titania.

She — Oh, that was nice. I remember. Queen Titania? Oh, yes, she was one of Shakespeare's characters, who fell in love with a man with a donkey's head.

He — H'm!

She — Now don't. I didn't mean you. Oh, Charles, listen to the Christmas chimes! What a merry day it will be for us. Are you sure you love me as well as you used to?

He	More. (*Smack.*)
She	Does 'em fink me sweet?
He	(*Smack. Smack!*)
She	Wuz 'em's toodleums?
He	Awful heap. Who do you wuv?
She	My ownest own old boy.
Both	(*Smack!*)
He	Listen, the bells are chiming again. We should be doubly happy, love, for we have passed through stormy seas of doubt and anger. But now, a light is breaking, and the rosy dawn of love has returned.
She	And should abide with us forever. Oh, Charles, let us never again by word or look cause pain to each other.
He	Never again. And you will not scold any more?
She	No, dearest. You know I never have unless you gave me cause.
He	Sometimes you have become angry and said hard things without any reason.
She	Maybe you think so, but I don't. (*Lifts her head from his shoulder.*)
He	I know what I'm talking about. (*Takes his arm from her waist.*)

She You come home cross because you haven't got sense enough to conduct your business properly, and take your spite out on me.

He You make me tired. You get on your ear because you are naturally one of the cain-raising, blab-mouthed kind and can't help it.

She You old crosspatch of a liar from Liarsville, don't you talk to me that way or I'll scratch your eyes out.

He You blamed wildcat. I wish I had been struck by lightning before I ever met you.

She (*Seizing the broom.*) Biff! biff! biff.

He (*After reaching the sidewalk*) I wonder if Colonel Ingersoll is right when he says suicide is no sin!

Curtain

Buying a Piano

A Houston man decided a few days ago to buy his wife a piano for a Christmas present. Now, there is more competition, rivalry, and push among piano agents than any other class of men. The insurance and fruit tree businesses are mild and retiring in comparison with the piano industry. The Houston man, who is a prominent lawyer, knew this, and he was careful not to tell too many people of his intentions, for fear the agents would annoy him. He inquired in a music store only once, regarding prices, etc., and intended after a week or so to make his selection.

When he left the store he went around by the post-office before going back to work.

When he reached his office he found three agents perched on his desk and in his chair waiting for him.

One of them got his mouth open first, and said: "Hear you want to buy a piano, sir. For sweetness, durability, finish, tone, workmanship, style, and quality the Steingay is—"

"Nixy," said another agent, pushing in between them and seizing the lawyer's collar. "You get a Chitterling. Only piano in the world. For sweetness, durability, finish, tone, workmanship—"

"Excuse me," said the third agent. "I can't stand by and see a man swindled. The Chronic and Bark piano, for sweetness, durability, finish—"

"Get out, every one of you," shouted the lawyer. "When I want a piano I'll buy the one I please. Get out of the room!"

The agents left, and the lawyer went to work on a brief. During the afternoon, five of his personal friends called to recommend different makes of pianos, and the lawyer began to get snappish.

He went out and got a drink and the bartender said: "Say, gent, me brudder works in a piano factory and he gimme de tip dat you'se wants to buy one of de tum-tums. Me brudder says dat for sweetness, durability, finish—"

"Devil take your brother," said the lawyer.

He got on the street car to go home and four agents were already aboard waiting for him. He dodged back before they saw him and stood on the platform. Presently the brakeman leaned over and whispered in his ear:

"Frien', the Epperson piano what me uncle handles in East Texas, fur sweetness, durability—"

"Stop the car," said the lawyer. He got off and skulked in a dark doorway until the four agents, who had also got off the car, rushed past, and then he picked up a big stone from the gutter and put it in his pocket. He went around a back way to his home and slipped up to the gate feeling pretty safe.

The minister of his church had been calling at the house, and came out the gate just as the lawyer reached it. The lawyer was the proud father of a brand-new, two-weeks-old baby, and the minister had just been admiring it, and wanted to congratulate him.

"My dear brother," said the minister. "Your house will soon be filled with joy and music. I think it will be a great addition to your life. Now, there is nothing in the world that for sweetness—"

"Confound you, you're drumming for a piano, too, are you?" yelled the lawyer, drawing the stone from his pocket. He fired away and knocked the minister's tall hat across the street, and kicked him in the shin. The minister believed in the church militant, and he gave the lawyer a one-two on the nose, and they clinched and rolled off the sidewalk on a pile of loose bricks. The neighbors heard the row and came out with shotguns and lanterns, and finally an understanding was arrived at.

The lawyer was considerably battered up, and the family doctor was sent for to patch him. As the doctor bent over him with sticking-plaster and a bottle of arnica, he said:

"You'll be out in a day or two, and then I want you to come around and buy a piano from my brother. The one he is agent for is acknowledged to be the best one for sweetness, durability, style, quality, and action in the world."

Too Late

Young Lieutenant Baldwin burst excitedly into his general's room and cried hoarsely: "For God's sake, General! Up! Up! and come. Spotted Lightning has carried off your daughter, Inez!"

General Splasher sprang to his feet in dismay. "What," he cried, "not Spotted Lightning, the chief of the Kiomas, the most peaceful tribe in the reservation?"

"The same."

"Good heavens! You know what this tribe is when aroused?"

The lieutenant cast a swift look of intelligence at his commander.

"They are the most revengeful, murderous, and vindictive Indians in the West when on the warpath, but for months they have been the most peaceable," he answered.

"Come," said the general, "we have not a moment to lose. What has been done?"

"There are fifty cavalrymen ready to start, with Bowie Knife Bill, the famous scout, to track them."

Ten minutes later the general and the lieutenant, with Bowie Knife Bill at their side, set out at a swinging gallop at the head of the cavalry column.

Bowie Knife Bill, with the trained instincts of a border sleuthhound, followed the trail of Spotted Lightning's horse with unerring swiftness.

"Pray God we may not be too late," said the general as he spurred his panting steed—"and Spotted Lightning, too, of all the chiefs! He has always seemed to be our friend."

"On, on," cried Lieutenant Baldwin, "there may yet be time."

Mile after mile the pursuers covered, pausing not for food or water, until nearly sunset.

Bowie Knife Bill pointed to a thin column of smoke in the distance and said:

"Thar's the varmints' camp."

The hearts of all the men bounded with excitement as they neared the spot.

"Are we in time?" was the silent question in the mind of each.

They dashed into an open space of prairie and drew rein near Spotted Lightning's tent. The flap was closed. The troopers swung themselves from their horses.

"If it is as I fear," muttered the general hoarsely to the lieutenant, "it means war with the Kioma nation. Oh, why did he not take some other instead of my daughter?"

At that instance the door of the tent opened and Inez Splasher, the general's daughter, a maiden of about thirty-seven summers, emerged, bearing in her hand the gory scalp of Spotted Lightning.

"Too late!" cried the general as he fell senseless from his horse.

"I knew it," said Bowie Knife Bill, folding his arms with a silent smile, "but what surprises me is how he ever got this far alive."

Nothing to Say

"You can tell your paper," the great man said,
"I refused an interview.
I have nothing to say on the question, sir,
Nothing to say to you."

And then he talked till the sun went down
And the chickens went to roost:
And he seized the coat of the poor *Post* man
And never his hold he loosed.

And the sun went down and the moon came up,
And he talked till the dawn of day;
Though he said, "On this subject mentioned by you,
I have nothing whatever to say."

And down the reporter dropped to sleep,
And flat on the floor he lay;
And the last he heard was the great man's words:
"I have nothing at all to say."

"Goin Home Fur Christmas"

Pa fussed at ma, and said By gun!
There wa'n't no use a talkin';
Times wuz too hard to travel round,
In any way 'cept walkin',
And said 'twas nonsense anyhow,
Folks didn't want no visitors;
And said ma needn't talk no more,
'Bout goin' home for Christmas.

"I'd like to see 'em all," says ma,
All pale and almost cryin';
A gazin' out the window, where
The snow wuz fairly flyin';
"I've been a thinkin', oh so long,
'Bout mother and my sisters;
And savin' every cent I could
To'ards goin' home for Christmas."
But pa he frowned and then ma sighed.
Just once, and kinder' smilin',
Says: "Well, les' go an' have some tea,
The water's all a-bilin'."

To-day pa called us children in
To ma's room—he wuz cryin'—
And ma wuz—oh so white and still,
And cold where she wuz lyin'.
She kinder roused up when we come,
And turned her face and kissed us,
And says: "Good-by—oh good-by, dears!
I'm goin' home fur Christmas!"

Just a Little Damp

As the steamer reached Aransas Pass a Galveston man fell overboard. A life buoy was thrown him, but he thrust it aside contemptuously. A boat was hurriedly lowered, and reached him just as he came to the surface for the second time. Helping hands were stretched forth to rescue him, but he spurned their aid. He spat out about a pint of sea water and shouted:

"Go away and leave me alone. I'm walking on the bottom. You'll run your boat aground in a minute. I'll wade out when I get ready and go up to a barber shop and get dusted off. The ground's damp a little, but I ain't afraid of catching cold."

He went under for the last time, and the boat pulled back for the ship. The Galveston man had exhibited to the last his scorn and contempt for any other port that claimed deep water.

Her Mysterious Charm

In the conservatory of a palatial Houston home Roland Pendergast stood with folded arms and an inscrutable smile upon his face, gazing down upon the upturned features of Gabrielle Smithers.

"Why is it," he said, "that I am attracted by you? You are not beautiful, you lack aplomb, grace, and savoir faire. You are cold, unsympathetic and bowlegged.

"I have striven to analyze the power you have over me, but in vain. Some esoteric chain of mental telepathy binds us two together, but what is its nature? I dislike being in love with one who has neither chic, naivete nor front teeth, but fate has willed it so. You personally repel me, but I can not tear you from my heart. You are in my thoughts by day and nightmares by night.

"Your form reminds me of a hatrack, but when I press you to my heart I feel strange thrills of joy. I can no more tell you why I love you than I can tell why a barber can rub a man's head fifteen minutes without touching the spot that itches. Speak, Gabrielle, and tell me what is this spell you have woven around me!"

"I will tell you," said Gabrielle with a soft smile. "I have fascinated many men in the same way. When I help you on with your overcoat I never reach under and try to pull your other coat down from the top of your collar."

Convinced

Houston is the dwelling place of a certain young lady who is exceptionally blessed with the gifts of the goddess of fortune. She is very fair to look upon, bright, witty, and possesses that gracious charm so difficult to describe, but so potent to please, that is commonly called personal magnetism. Although cast in such a lonely world, and endowed with so many graces of mind and matter, she is no idle butterfly of fashion, and the adulation she receives from a numerous circle of admirers has not turned her head.

She has a close friend, a young lady of plain exterior, but a sensible and practical mind, whom she habitually consults as a wise counselor and advisor concerning the intricate problems of life.

One day she said to Marian—the wise friend: "How I wish there was some way to find out who among these flattering suitors of mine is sincere and genuine in the compliments that are paid me. Men are such deceivers, and they all give me such unstinted praise, and make such pretty speeches to me, that I do not know who among them, if any, are true and sincere in their regard."

"I will tell you a way," said Marian. "The next evening when there are a number of them calling upon you, recite a dramatic poem, and then tell me how each one expresses his opinion of your effort."

The young lady was much impressed with the idea, and on the following Friday evening when some half-dozen young men were in the parlor paying her attentions, she volunteered to recite. She has not the least dramatic talent, but she stood up and went through with a long poem, with many gestures and much rolling of eyes and pressing of her hands to her heart. She did it very badly, and without the least regard for the rules of elocution or expression.

Later on, her friend Marian asked her how her effort was received.

"Oh," she said, "they all crowded around me, and appeared to be filled with the utmost delight. Tom, and Henry, and Jim, and Charlie were in raptures. They said that Mary Anderson could not have equaled it. They said they had never heard anything spoken with such dramatic effect and feeling."

"Everyone praised you?" asked Marian.

"All but one. Mr. Judson sat back in his chair and never applauded at all. He told me after I had finished that he was afraid I had very little dramatic talent at all."

"Now," said Marian. "You know who is sincere and genuine?"

"Yes," said the beautiful girl, with eyes shining with enthusiasm. "The test was a complete success. I detest that odious Judson, and I'm going to begin studying for the stage right away."

His Dilemma

An old man with long white chin whiskers and a derby hat two sizes small, dropped into a Main Street drug store yesterday and beckoned a clerk over into a corner. He was about sixty-five years old, but he wore a bright red necktie, and was trying to smoke a very bad and strong cigar in as offhand a style as possible.

"Young man," he said, "you lemme ask you a few questions, and I'll send you a big watermelon up from the farm next summer. I came to Houston to see this here carnival, and do some tradin'. Right now, before I go any further, have you got any hair dye?"

"Plenty of it."

"Any of this real black shiny dye that looks blue in the sunshine?"

"Yes."

"All right then, now I'll proceed. Do you know anything about this here Monroe docterin'?"

"Well, yes, something."

"And widders; do you feel able to prognosticate a few lines about widders?"

"I can't tell what you are driving at," said the clerk. "What is it you want to know?"

"I'm gettin' to the pint. Now there's hair dye, Monroe docterin', and widders. Got them all down in your mind?"

"Yes, but—"

"Jest hold on, now, and I'll explain. There's the unhappiest fat and sassy widder moved into the adjinin' farm to me, you ever see, and if I knows the female heart she has cast eyes of longin' upon yours truly. Now if I dyes these here white whiskers I ketches her. By blackin' said whiskers and insertin' say four fingers of rye where it properly belongs, I kicks up my heels and I waltzes up and salutes the widder like a calf of forty."

"Well," said the clerk, "our hair dye is—"

"Wait a minute, young feller. Now on the other hand I hears rumors of wars this mornin', and I hears alarmin' talk about this here Monroe docterin'. Ef I uses hair dye and trains down to thirty-eight or forty years of age, I ketches the widder, but I turns into a peart and chipper youth what is liable to be made to fight in this here great war. Ef I gives up the hair dye, the recrutin' sargent salutes these white hairs and passes by, but I am takin' big chances on the widder. She has been to meetin' twicet with a man what has been divorced, and ties his own cree-vat, and this here Monroe docterin' is all what keeps me from pulling out seventy-five cents and makin' a strong play with said dye. What would you do, ef you was me, young feller?"

"I don't think there will be any war soon," said the clerk.

"Jerusalem; I'm glad to hear it! Gimme the biggest bottle of blue-black hair dye fur seventy-five cents that you got. I'm goin' to purpose to that widder before it gets dry, and risk the chances of Monroe takin' water again on this war business."

Something for Baby

This is nothing but a slight jar in the happy holiday music; a minor note struck by the finger of Fate, slipping upon the keys, as anthems of rejoicing and Christmas carols make the Yuletide merry.

The Post man stood yesterday in one of the largest fancy and drygoods stores on Main Street, watching the throng of well-dressed buyers, mostly ladies, who were turning over the stock of Christmas notions and holiday goods.

Presently a little, slim, white-faced girl crept timidly through the crowd to the counter. She was dressed in thin calico, and her shoes were patched and clumsy.

She looked about her with a manner half mournful, half scared.

A clerk saw her and came forward.

"Well, what is it?" he asked rather shortly.

"Please, sir," she answered in a weak voice, "Mamma gave me this dime to get something for baby."

"Something for baby, for a dime? Want to buy baby a Christmas present, eh? Well now, don't you think you had better run around to a toyshop? We don't keep such things here. You want a tin horse, or a ball, or a jumping jack, now don't you?"

"Please, sir, Mamma said I was to come here. Baby isn't with us now. Mamma told me to get—ten—cents—worth—of—crape, sir, if you please."

Some Day

Some day—not now; oh, ask me not again;
Impassioned, low, and deep, with wild regret;
Thy words but fill my heart with haunting pain—
Some day, but oh, my friend—not yet—not yet.

Perchance when time hath wrought some wondrous change,
And fate hath swept her barriers away.
Then, lifted to some higher, freer range.
Thou may'st return and speak again—some day.

Oh, leave me now—do not so coldly turn!
Thou seest my very soul has suffered sore.
Adieu! But, oh, some day thou canst return
And bring that drygoods bill to me once more.

A Green Hand

"I shall never again employ any but experienced salesmen, who thoroughly understand the jewelry business," said a Houston jeweler to a friend yesterday.

"You see, at Christmas time we generally need more help, and sometimes employ people who can sell goods, but are not familiar with the fine points of the business. Now, that young man over there is thoroughly good and polite to everyone, but he has just lost me one of my best customers."

"How was that?" asked the friend.

"A man who always trades with us came in with his wife last week and with her assistance selected a magnificent diamond pin that he had promised her for a Christmas present and told this young man to lay it aside for him till today."

"I see," said the friend, "and he sold it to someone else and disappointed him."

"It's plain you don't know much about married men," said the jeweler. "That idiot of a clerk actually saved the pin for him and he had to buy it."

A Righteous Outburst

He smelled of gin and his whiskers resembled the cylinder of a Swiss music box. He walked into a toy shop on Main Street yesterday and leaned sorrowfully against the counter.

"Anything today?" asked the proprietor coldly.

He wiped an eye with a dingy red handkerchief and said:

"Nothing at all, thank you. I just came inside to shed a tear. I do not like to obtrude my grief upon the passersby. I have a little daughter, sir; five years of age, with curly golden hair. Her name is Lilian. She says to me this morning: 'Papa, will Santa Claus bring me a red wagon for Christmas?' It completely unmanned me, sir, as, alas, I am out of work and penniless. Just think, one little red wagon would bring her happiness, and there are children who have hundreds of red wagons."

"Before you go out," said the proprietor, "which you are going to do in about fifteen seconds, I am willing to inform you that I have a branch store on Trains Street, and was around there yesterday. You came in and made the same talk about your little girl, whom you called Daisy, and I gave you a wagon. It seems you don't remember your little girl's name very well."

The man drew himself up with dignity, and started for the door. When nearly there, he turned and said:

"Her name is Lilian Daisy, sir, and the wagon you gave me had a rickety wheel and some of the paint was scratched off the handle. I have a friend who tends bar on Willow Street, who is keeping it for me till Christmas, but I will feel a flush of shame on your behalf, sir, when Lilian Daisy sees that old, slab-sided, squeaking, secondhand, leftover-from-last-year's-stock wagon. But, sir, when Lilian Daisy kneels at her little bed at night I shall get her to pray for you, and ask Heaven to have mercy on you. Have you one of your business cards handy, so Lilian Daisy can get your name right in her petitions?"

Getting at the Facts

It was late in the afternoon and the day staff was absent. The night editor had just come in, pulled off his coat, vest, collar, and necktie, rolled up his shirtsleeves and eased down his suspenders, and was getting ready for work.

Someone knocked timidly outside the door, and the night editor yelled, "Come in."

A handsome young lady with entreating blue eyes and a Psyche knot entered with a rolled manuscript in her hand.

The night editor took it silently and unrolled it. It was a poem and he read it half aloud with a convulsive jaw movement that resulted from his organs of speech being partially engaged with about a quarter of a plug of chewing tobacco. The poem ran thus:

A Requiem

The soft, sweet, solemn dawn stole through
The latticed room's deep gloom;
He lay in pallid, pulseless peace,
Fulfilled his final doom.
Oh, breaking heart of mine—oh, break!
Left lonely here to mourn;
My alter ego, mentor, friend
Thus from me rudely torn.
Within his chamber dead he lies,
And stilled is his sweet lyre;
How long he pored o'er midnight oil.
With grand poetic fire!
Till came the crash, when his bright light
Went out, and all was drear;
And my sad soul was left to wait
In grief and anguish here.

"When did this happen?" asked the night editor.

"I wrote it last night, sir," said the young lady. "Is it good enough to print?"

"Last night! H'm. A little stale, but the other papers didn't get it. Now, miss," continued the night editor, smiling and throwing out his chest, "I'm going to teach you a lesson in the newspaper business. We can use this item, but it's not in proper shape. Just take that chair, and I'll rewrite it for you, showing you how to properly condense a news item in order to secure its insertion."

The young lady seated herself and the night editor knitted his brows and read over the poem two or three times to get the main points. He then wrote a few lines upon a sheet of paper and said:

"Now, miss, here is the form in which your item will appear when we print it:

> Fatal Accident
>
> "Last evening Mr. Alter Ego of this city was killed by the explosion of a kerosene lamp while at work in his room.

"Now, you see, miss, the item includes the main facts in the case, and—"

"Sir!" said the young lady indignantly. "There is nothing of the kind intimated in the poem. The lines are imaginary and are intended to express the sorrow of a poet's friend at his untimely demise."

"Why, miss," said the night editor, "it plainly refers to midnight oil, and a crash, and when the light blew up the gent was left for dead in the room."

"You horrid thing," said the young lady, "give me my manuscript. I will bring it back when the literary editor is in."

"I'm sorry," said the night editor as he handed her the roll. "We're short on news tonight, and it would have made a nice little scoop. Don't happen to know of any accidents in your ward: births, runaways, holdups, or breach of promise suits, do you?"

But the slamming of the door was the only answer from the fair poetess.

Just for a Change

The "lullaby boy" to the same old tune,
Who abandons his drum and toys,
For the purpose of dying in early June,
Is the kind the public enjoys.

But, just for a change please sing us a song,
Of the sore-toed boy that's fly,
And freckled, and mean, and ugly, and strong,
And positively will not die.

Too Wise

Here is a man in Houston who keeps quite abreast of the times. He reads the papers, has traveled extensively and is an excellent judge of human nature. He has a natural gift for detecting humbugs and fakirs, and it would be a smooth artist indeed who could impose upon him in any way.

Last night as he was going home, a shady looking man with his hat pulled over his eyes stepped out from a doorway and said:

"Say, gent, here's a fine diamond ring I found in de gutter. I don't want to get into no trouble wid it. Gimme a dollar and take it."

The Houston man smiled as he looked at the flashy ring the man held toward him.

"A very good game, my man," he said, "but the police are hot after you fellows. You had better select your rhinestone customers with better judgment. Good night."

When the man got home he found his wife in tears.

"Oh, John," she said. "I went shopping this afternoon and lost my solitaire diamond ring. Oh, what shall I—"

John turned without a word and rushed back down the street, but the shady-looking man was not to be found.

His wife often wonders why he never scolded her for losing the ring.

A Fatal Error

"What are you looking so glum about?" asked a Houston man as he dropped into a friend's office on Christmas Day.

"Same old fool break of putting a letter in the wrong envelope, and I'm afraid to go home. My wife sent me down a note by the hired man an hour ago, telling me to send her ten dollars, and asking me to meet her here at the office at three o'clock and go shopping with her. At the same time I got a bill for ten dollars from a merchant I owe, asking me to remit. I scribbled off a note to the merchant saying: 'Can't possibly do it. I've got to meet another little thing today that won't be put off.' I made the usual mistake and sent the merchant the ten dollars and my wife the note."

"Can't you go home and explain the mistake to your wife?"

"You don't know her. I've done all I can. I've taken out an accident policy for $10,000 good for two hours, and I expect her here in fifteen minutes. Tell all the boys goodbye for me, and if you meet a lady on the stairs as you go down keep close to the wall."

Prompt

He raised his arm to strike, but lax and slow
His arm fell nerveless to his side.
He might have struck a mighty ringing blow.
A blow that might have been his joy and pride.

But no—his strength at once did fade away,
A sudden blow seemed all his soul to fix;
He was a workman, working by the day,
And heard the whistle blow the hour of six.

The Rake-Off

"Who bids?"

The auctioneer held up a child's rocking-horse, battered and stained. It had belonged to some little member of the man's family whose household property was being sold under the hammer.

He was utterly ruined. He had given up everything in the world to his creditors—house, furniture, horses, stock of goods and lands. He stood among the crowd watching the sale that was scattering his household goods and his heirlooms among a hundred strange hands.

On his arm leaned a woman heavily veiled. "Who bids?"

The auctioneer held the rocking-horse high that it might be seen. Childish hands had torn away the scanty mane; the bridle was twisted and worn by tender little fingers. The crowd was still.

The woman under the heavy veil sobbed and stretched out her hands.

"No, no, no!" she cried.

The man was white with emotion. The little form that once so merrily rode the old rockinghouse had drifted away into the world years ago. This was the only relic left of his happy infancy.

The auctioneer, with a queer moisture in his eyes, handed the rocking-horse to the man without a word. He seized it with eager hands, and he and the veiled woman hurried away.

The crowd murmured with sympathy.

The man and the woman went into an empty room and set the rocking-horse down. He took out his knife, ripped open the front of the horse, and took out a roll of bills. He counted them and said: "It's a cold day when I fail without a rake-off. Eight thousand five hundred dollars, but that auctioneer came very near busting up the game."

The Telegram

Scene: Telegraph office in Houston.

Enter handsome black velour cape, trimmed with jet and braid, with Tibetan fur collar, all enclosing lovely young lady.

Young lady — Oh, I want to send a telegram at once, if you please. Give me about six blanks, please. (*Writes about ten minutes.*) How much will this amount to, please?

Clerk — (*counting words*) Sixteen dollars and ninety-five cents, ma'am.

Young lady — Goodness gracious! I've only thirty cents with me. *Suspiciously*. How is it you charge so much, when the post-office only requires two cents?

Clerk — We claim to deliver messages quicker than the post-office, ma'am. You can send ten words to Waco for twenty-five cents.

Young lady — Give me another blank, please: I guess that will be enough. (*After five minutes' hard work she produces the following: "Ring was awfully lovely. Come down as soon as you can. Mamie."*)

Clerk — This contains eleven words. That will be thirty cents.

Young lady — Oh, gracious! I wanted that nickel to buy gum with.

Clerk — Let's see. You might strike out, "awfully," and that will make it all right.

Young lady — Indeed I shan't. You ought to see that ring. I'll give you the thirty cents.

Clerk — To whom is this to be sent?

Young lady — It seems to me you are rather inquisitive, sir.

Clerk — (*wearily*) I assure you there is no personal interest expressed in the question. We have to know the name and address in order to send the message.

Young lady	Oh, yes. I didn't think of that. (*She writes the name and address, pays the thirty cents and departs. Twenty minutes later she returns, out of breath.*)
Young lady	Oh, I forgot something. Have you sent it off yet?
Clerk	Yes, ten minutes ago.
Young lady	Oh, I'm so sorry. It isn't the way I wanted it at all. Can't you telegraph and have it changed for me?
Clerk	Is it anything important?
Young lady	Yes: I wanted to underscore the words "awfully lovely." Will you have that attended to at once?
Clerk	Certainly, and we have some real nice violet extract; would you like a few drops on your telegram?
Young lady	Oh, yes: so kind of you. I expect to send all my telegrams through your office, you have been so accommodating. Good morning.

An Opportunity Declined

A farmer who lives about four miles from Houston noticed a stranger in his front yard one afternoon last week acting in a rather unusual manner. He wore a pair of duck trousers stuffed in his boots, and had a nose the color of Elgin pressed brick. In his hand he held a sharpened stake about two feet long, which he would stick into the ground, and after sighting over it at various objects would pull it up and go through the same performance at another place.

The farmer went out in the yard and inquired what he wanted.

"Wait just a minute," said the stranger, squinting his eye over the stick at the chicken house. "Now, that's it to a *T*. You see, I'm one of de odnance corps of engineers what's runnin' de line of the new railroad from Columbus, Ohio, to Houston. See? De other fellers is over de hill wid de transit and de baggage. Dere's over a million dollars in de company. See? Dey sent me on ahead to locate a place for a big passenger depot, to cost $27,000. De foundation will commence right by your chicken house. Say, I gives you a pointer. You charge 'em high for dis land. Dey'll stand fifty thousand. 'Cause why? 'Cause dey's got de money and dey's got to build de depot right where I says. See? I've got to go on into Houston to record a deed for a right of way, and I never thought to get fifty cents from de treasurer. He's a little man with light pants. You might let me have de fifty cents and when de boys comes along in de mornin' tell 'em what you did, and any one of 'em' hand you a dollar. You might ask 'em fifty-five thousand, if you—"

"You throw that stick over the fence, and get the axe and cut up exactly half a cord of that wood, stove length, and I'll give you a quarter and your supper," said the farmer. "Does the proposition strike you favorably?"

"And are you goin' to t'row away de opportunity of havin' dat depot built right here, and sellin' out—"

"Yes, I need the ground for my chicken coop."

"You refuse to take $50,000 for de ground, den?"

"I do. Are you going to chop that wood, or shall I whistle for Tige?"

"Gimme dat axe, mister, and show me dat wood, and tell de missus to bake an extra pan of biscuits for supper. When dat Columbus and Houston grand trunk railway runs up against your front fence you'll be sorry you didn’t take up dat offer. And tell her to fill up the molasses pitcher, too, and not to mind about putting the dish of cooking butter on de table. See?”

Correcting a Great Injustice

Something has been recently disclosed that will fill every chivalrous man in the country with contrition. For a long time men have supposed that the habit of wearing tall hats at the theater by the ladies was nothing more than a lack of consideration on their part for the unfortunate individuals who were so unlucky as to get a seat behind them.

It now appears that the supposition did the fair sex a great injustice. A noted female physician has exposed an affliction that the female sex has long suffered with, and have succeeded up to this time in keeping a profound secret. Their habit of wearing hats in places of public entertainment is the result of a necessity, and relieves them of the charge of selfish disregard of the convenience of others, which has been so often brought against them.

It appears that ladies who are past thirty-five years of age are peculiarly sensitive to the effect of a bright light striking upon their heads from above. The skull of a woman is quite different from that of a man, especially on the top, and at the age of thirty-five, the texture of the skull at this place becomes very light. Rays of light—especially electric light—have a peculiarly penetrating and disturbing effect upon the cerebral nerves.

Strange to say, this infirmity is never felt by a young woman, but as soon as she passes the heyday of youth, it is at once perceptible. The fact is generally known to women, and discussed among themselves, but they have jealously guarded the secret, even from their nearest male relatives and friends. The lady physician who recently exposed the matter in a scientific journal is the first of her sex to make it known to the public.

If anyone will take the trouble to make a test of the statement, its truth will be unquestionably proven. Engage a woman of middle age in conversation beneath a well-lighted chandelier, and in a few moments she will grow uneasy, and very soon the pain inflicted by the light will cause her to move away from under its source. On young and healthy girls the rays of light have no perceptible effect. So, when we see a lady at a theater wearing a tall and cumbersome hat, we should reflect that she is more than thirty-five years old, and is simply protecting herself from an affliction that advancing years have brought upon her. Whenever we observe one wearing small and unobtrusive headgear we know that she is still young and charming, and can yet sit beneath the rays of penetrating light without inconvenience.

No man who has had occasion to rail against woman's supposed indifference to the public comfort in this respect, will hesitate to express sincere regret that he has so misunderstood them. It is characteristic of Americans to respect the infirmities of age, especially among the fair sex, and when the facts here narrated have been generally known, pity and toleration will take the place of censure. Henceforth a tall hat, with nodding feathers and clustering flowers and trimming, will not be regarded with aversion when we see it between us and the stage, but with respect, since we are assured that its wearer is no longer young, but is already on the down hill of life, and is forced to take the precaution that advancing years render necessary to infirm women.

A Startling Demonstration

What a terrible state of affairs it would be if we could read each other's minds! It is safe to say that if such were the case, most of us would be afraid to think above a whisper.

As an illustration, a case might be cited that occurred in Houston. Some months ago a very charming young lady came to this city giving exhibitions in mind reading, and proved herself to be marvelously gifted in that respect. She easily read the thoughts of the audience, finding many articles hidden by simply holding the hand of the person secreting them, and read sentences written on little slips of paper by some at a considerable distance from her.

A young man in Houston fell in love with her, and married her after a short courtship. They went to housekeeping and for a time were as happy as mortals can be.

One evening they were sitting on the porch of their residence holding each other's hands, and wrapt in the close communion of mutual love, when she suddenly rose and knocked him down the steps with a large flowerpot. He arose astonished, with a big bump on his head, and asked her, if it were not too much trouble, to explain.

"You can't fool me," she said with flashing eyes. "You were thinking of a redheaded girl named Maud with a gold plug in her front tooth and a light pink waist and a black silk skirt on Rusk Avenue, standing under a cedar bush chewing gum at twenty minutes to eight with your arm around her waist and calling her 'sweetness,' while she fooled with your watch chain and said: 'Oh, George, give me a chance to breathe,' and her mother was calling her to supper. Don't you dare to deny it. Now, when you can get your mind on something better than that, you can come in the house and not before."

Then the door slammed and George and the broken flowerpot were alone.

Leap Year Advice

Spinsters must be up and doing: 1896 will be the only leap year for the next eight years. Once in every four years the wise men who made the calendar insert an extra day so that the average year will not be so short. Once in every hundred years this extra day is omitted, and a leap year is also dropped. The year 1900 will not be a leap year. Unmarried ladies who yearn for matrimonial chains, and have been left standing in the comer by fickle man must get to work. If they fail in landing their prize during 1896 they will have to wait eight years more before they can propose again. Therefore they should work early and late during the present year.

The following communication pertaining to the subject was received yesterday.

> Houston, Texas, January 1, 1896.
>
> The Houston Post.
>
> *Gentlemen*: This being leap year I arose this morning at daybreak, resolved to utilize every moment of the time possible. Four years ago, I wrote and received some very valuable advice from you in regard to the exercise of the privileges of my sex (female) during the leap year season. I followed your advice strictly, and in the year 1892 proposed marriage to twenty-seven different men. I am still single, but am not to blame for that. I was engaged to three men in 1892, and, but for the unforeseen bad luck, would certainly have married at least one of them. Two of them committed suicide the day before the wedding and the other got his hat and walking cane and went to Patagonia. I see in the papers that the year 1900 will not be a leap year, and I realize that for the next twelve months I have got to carry on a red hot aggressive campaign, as eight more years will decidedly weaken my chances. Any suggestions you may make that will aid me will be appreciated. I enclose my photo. I am nearly thirty-six, and sleep on my left side.
>
> Faithfully yours,
>
> Bettie Louis M——

This is an awful subject to speak lightly upon, and the few words of advice we propose giving are sincere and well weighed.

Your photograph shows that whatever you do must be done quickly. A good way for a lady of your age and cut of collar bones to open New Year would be with prayer and massage. It may be a defect in the retouching of your photo, but still, it would not be amiss to take a good Turkish bath and then go over low places with plaster of Paris applied with a common case knife with gentle downward motion, breathing as usual, and dry in the sun, turning over frequently two or three hours before eating. You should not waste any time in selecting a man. Try the milkman first, as he generally comes before it is very light.

As the milkman will no doubt refuse you, be prepared to give the postman a shock. Do not be too abrupt in proposing, as a rude shock of this nature will often cause a timid man to stampede, causing great loss of confidence and bric-a-brac.

After getting a victim to stand, speak gently to him until he ceases to quiver in his limbs and roll his eyes. Do not pat his chest, or rub his nose, as men will sometimes kick at this treatment. Bear in mind the fact that 1900 is not leap year, and keep between him and the door.

Approach the subject gradually, allowing him no time to pray and remove the cigars from his vest pocket. If he should shudder and turn pale, turn the conversation upon progressive euchre, Braun's egotism, or some other light subject, until a handkerchief applied to his neck will not come off wet. If possible, get him to seat himself, and then, grasping both lapels of his coat, breathe heavily upon him, and speak of your lonely life.

At this stage he will mutter incoherently, answer at random, and try to climb up the chimney. When his pulse gets to 195, and he begins to babble of green fields and shows only the whites of his eyes, strike him on the point of the chin, propose, chloroform him, and telephone for a minister.

After Supper

Mr. Sharp: "My darling, it seems to me that every year that passes over your head but brings out some new charm, some hidden beauty, some added grace. There is a look in your eyes tonight that is as charming and girllike as when I first met you. What a blessing it is when two hearts can grow but fonder as time flies. You are scarcely less beautiful now than when—"

Mrs. Sharp: "I had forgotten it was lodge night, Robert. Don't be out much after twelve, if you can help it."

His Only Opportunity

Last week "The Rainmakers" gave two performances in Houston. At the night performance a prominent local politician occupied one of the front seats, as near to the stage as possible. He carried in his hand a glossy silk hat, and he seemed to be in a state of anxious suspense, fidgeting about in his chair, and holding his hat in both hands straight before him. A friend who occupied a seat directly behind, leaned over and asked the cause of his agitation.

"I'll tell you, Bill," said the politician in a confidential whisper, "just how it is. I've been in politics now for ten years, and I've been bemoaned and abused and cussed out, and called so many hard names that I thought I'd like to be addressed in a decent manner once more before I die, and this is about the only opportunity I shall have. There is a sleight-of-hand performance between two of the acts in this show, and the professor is going to step down to the front and say: 'Will some gentleman kindly loan me a hat?' Then I'm going to stand up and give him mine, and it'll make me feel good for a week. I haven't been called a gentleman in so long. I expect I'll whoop right out hard when he takes the hat. Excuse me now. I've got to be ready and get my hat in first. I see one of the city councilmen over there with an old derby in his hand, and I'll bet he's up to the same game."

Getting Acquainted

His coat was rusty and his hat out of style, but his nose glasses, secured by a black cord, lent him a distinguished air, and his manner was jaunty and assured. He stepped into a new Houston grocery yesterday, and greeted the proprietor cordially.

"I'll have to introduce myself," he said. "My name is ———, and I live next door to the house you have just moved in. Saw you at church Sunday. Our minister also observed you, and after church he says, 'Brother ———, you must really find out who that intelligent-looking stranger is who listened so attentively today.' How did you like the sermon?"

"Very well," said the grocer as he picked some funny-looking currants with wings out of a jar.

"Yes, he is a very eloquent and pious man. You have not been in business long in Houston, have you?"

"Three weeks," said the grocer, as he removed the cheese knife from the box to the shelf behind him.

"Our people," said the rusty-looking man, "are whole-souled and hospitable. There is no welcome too warm for them to extend to a newcomer, and the members of our church in particular are especially friendly toward anyone who drops in to worship with us. You have a nice stock of goods."

"So, so," said the grocer, turning his back and gazing up at a supply of canned California fruits.

"Only last week now I had quite an altercation with the tradesman I deal with for sending me inferior goods. You have some nice hams, I suppose, and such staples as coffee and sugar?"

"Yep," said the grocer.

"My wife was over to see your wife this morning, and enjoyed her visit very much. What time does your delivery wagon pass up our street?"

"Say," said the grocer. "I bought out an old stock of groceries here, and put in a lot of new ones. I see your name on the old books charged with $87.10 balance on account. Did you want something more today?"

"No, sir," said the rusty man, drawing himself up and glaring through his glasses. "I merely called in from a sense of Christian duty to extend you a welcome, but I see you are not the man I took you to be. I don't want any of your groceries. I can see the mites in that cheese from the other side of the street, and my wife says your wife is wearing an underskirt made out of an old tablecloth. Several of our congregation were speaking of your smelling of toddy in church, and snoring during the prayers. My wife will return that cup of lard she borrowed at your house this morning just as quick as my last order comes up from the store where we trade. Good morning, sir."

The grocer softly whispered, "There Won't Anybody Play with Me," and whittled a little lead out of one of his weights, in an absentminded way.

Answers to Inquiries

> *Dear Editor*: I want to ask a question in arithmetic. I am a school boy and am anxious to know the solution. If my pa, who keeps a grocery on Milam Street, sells four cans of tomatoes for twenty-five cents, and twenty-two pounds of sugar, and one can of extra evaporated apples and three cans of superior California plums, for only—

There! There! little boy; that will do. Tell your pa to come around and see the advertising manager, who is quite an arithmetician, and will doubtless work the sum for you at the usual rates.

City Perils

Jeremiah Q. Dilworthy lives away up on San Jacinto Street. He walks home every night. On January first, he promised his wife he would not take another drink in a year. He forgot his promise and on Tuesday night we met some of the boys, and when he started home about nine o'clock he was feeling a trifle careless.

Mr. Dilworthy was an old resident of Houston, and on rainy nights he always walked in the middle of the street, which is well paved.

Alas! if Mr. Dilworthy had only remembered the promise made his wife!

He started out all right, and just as he was walking up San Jacinto Street he staggered over to one side of the street.

A policeman standing on the comer heard a loud yell of despair, and turning, saw a man throw up his arms and then disappear from sight. Before the policeman could call someone who could swim the man had gone for the third and last time.

Mr. Jeremiah Q. Dilworthy had fallen into the sidewalk.

Hush Money

He was a great practical joker, and never lost a chance to get a good one on somebody. A few days ago he stopped a friend on Main Street and said, confidentially:

"I never would have believed it, but I believe it my duty to make it known. Mr. ———, the alderman for our ward, has been taking hush money."

"Impossible!" said his friend.

"I tell you, it's true, for I overheard the conversation and actually saw it handed over to him, and he took the money and put it in his pocket."

Then he went on without explaining any further, and the thing got talked around considerably for a day or two.

He forgot all about it until one day he met the alderman and suffered from the encounter to the extent of two black eyes and a coat split up the back.

And then he had to go all round and explain that what he meant was that he had seen the alderman's wife give him a dime to buy some paregoric for the baby.

Relieved

A Houston gentleman who is worth somewhere up in the hundreds of thousands and lives on eleven dollars a week, was sitting in his private office a few days ago, when a desperate looking man entered and closed the door carefully behind him. The man had an evil, villainous-looking face, and in his hand he held with the utmost care an oblong, square-shaped package. "What do you want?" asked the capitalist.

"I must have money," hissed the stranger. "I am starving while you are rolling in wealth. Do you see this little package? Do you know what it contains?"

The wealthy citizen sprang from his desk in horror, pale with fright.

"No, no," he gasped. "You would not be so cruel, so heartless."

"This package," continued the desperate man, "contains enough dynamite, if let fall upon the floor, to hurl this building into a shapeless mass of ruins."

"Is that all?" said the capitalist, sinking into his chair and picking up his newspaper with a sigh of relief. "You don't know how much you frightened me. I thought it was a gold brick."

No Time to Lose

A young Houston mother rushed into die house the other day in the utmost excitement, calling out to her mother to put an iron on the fire as quick as possible.

"What is the matter?" asked the old lady.

"A dog has just bitten Tommy, and I am afraid it was mad. Oh, hurry up, mother; be as quick as you can!"

"Are you going to try to cauterize the wound?"

"No—I've got to iron that blue skirt before I can wear it to go after the doctor. Do be in a hurry."

A Villainous Trick

When it becomes necessary for an actor to write a letter during the performance of a play, it is a custom to read the words aloud as he writes them. It is necessary to do this in order that the audience may be apprised of its contents, otherwise the clearness of the plot might be obscured. The writing of a letter upon the stage, therefore, generally has an important bearing upon the situation being presented, and of course the writer is forced to read aloud what he writes for the benefit of the audience. During the production of "Monbars" in Houston some days ago, the gentleman who assumed the character of the heavy villain took advantage of a situation of this description in a most cowardly manner.

In the last act, Mantell, as Monbars, writes a letter of vital importance, and, as customary, reads the lines aloud as he writes them. The villain hides behind the curtains of a couch and listens in fiendish glee to the contents of the letter as imparted by Mr. Mantell in strict confidence to the audience. He then uses the information obtained in this underhanded manner to further his own devilish designs.

Mr. Mantell ought not to allow this. A man who is a member of his own company, and who, no doubt is drawing a good salary, should be above taking a mean advantage of a mere stage technicality.

A Forced March

The young man is a-walking with his girl
Hear him swear
That he loves her and adores her.
And he woos her, and, of course, her
Little foolish heart doth force her;
She's half crazy and her thoughts are in a whirl.

The young man is a-walking with his girl.
(Hear him swear.)
She is two months old and screaming,
While around the room he's steaming,
And her ma is in bed dreaming;
He's half crazy and his thoughts are in a whirl.

Book Reviews

Unabridged Dictionary by Noah Webster, L. L. D. F. R. S. X. Y. Z.

We find on our table quite an exhaustive treatise on various subjects, written in Mr. Webster's well-known, lucid, and piquant style. There is not a dull line between the covers of the book. The range of subjects is wide, and the treatment light and easy without being flippant. A valuable feature of the work is the arranging of the articles in alphabetical order, thus facilitating the finding of any particular word desired. Mr. Webster's vocabulary is large, and he always uses the right word in the right place. Mr. Webster's work is thorough and we predict that he will be heard from again.

Houston's City Directory, by Morrison and Fourmy.

This new book has the decided merit of being non-sensational. In these days of erratic and ultra-imaginative literature of the modern morbid self-analytical school it is a relief to peruse a book with so little straining after effect, so well balanced, and so pure in sentiment. It is a book that a man can place in the hands of the most innocent member of his family with the utmost confidence. Its material is healthy, and its literary style excellent, as it adheres to the methods used with such thrilling effect by Mr. Webster in his famous dictionary, viz: alphabetical arrangement.

We venture to assert that no one can carefully and conscientiously read this little volume without being a better man, or lady, as circumstances over which they have no control may indicate.

A Conditional Pardon

The runaway couple had just returned, and she knelt at the old man's feet and begged forgiveness.

"Yes, forgive us," cried the newly wedded husband. "Forgive me for taking her away from you, but see, I have brought her back."

"Yes," said the old man, his voice trembling with emotion, "you have brought her back. You have brought her back. Bat that is not all, lad; you have brought her back, but you have also brought the part of her that eats provisions. I will forgive you for fifty dollars per month, lights and washing extra."

It is but justice to the Pension Bureau at Washington to state that they have not yet granted the pension claimed by a man who was wounded in the late unpleasantness by the accidental discharge of his duty.

A careful inquiry has revealed the fact that Samson was the first man who rushed the growler.

Better blow your own horn than one you haven't paid for.

If your rye offend you, buy a better quality.

Inconsistency

Call a pretty girl a witch
And she'll do her best to charm you.
Tell an old maid she's a witch,
And she certainly will harm you.
Thus you see how hard it is to please them all.

Call a pretty maiden "Puss,"
And she'll archly smile upon you.
Call an ancient one a "cat,"
She will grab an axe and run you.
The same name will not fit them all, at all.

If you call your girl a "mouse,"
She will think it cute and pretty.
If unto an aged spinster

You say "rats," you have our pity.
Thus you see you need not try to please them all.

"In a lighthouse by the sea" is what the opera company sang to a forty-dollar audience in Galveston.

"Yes," said the tramp as he accepted the dime and made for the lunch counter, "I always hollers when I'm hit and I always hits a man when I'm holler."

Bill Nye

Bill Nye, who recently laid down his pen for all time, was a unique figure in the field of humor. His best work probably more nearly represented American humor than that of any other writer. Mr. Nye had a sense of ludicrous that was keen and judicious. His humor was peculiarly American in that it depended upon sharp and unexpected contrasts, and the bringing of opposites into unlooked-for comparison for its effect. Again, he had the true essence of kindliness, without which humor is stripped of its greatest component part.

Bill Nye's jokes never had a sting. They played like summer lightning around the horizon of life, illuminating and spreading bright, if transitory, pictures upon the sky, but they were as harmless as the smile of a child. The brain of the man conceived the swift darts that he threw, but his great manly heart broke off their points.

He knew human nature as a scholar knows his book, and the knowledge did not embitter him. He saw all the goodness in frailty, and his clear eyes penetrated the frailty of goodness.

His was the child's heart, the scholar's knowledge, and the philosopher's view of life. He might have won laurels in other fields, for he was a careful reasoner, and a close observer, but he showed his greatness in putting aside cold and fruitless discussions that have wearied the world long ago, and set himself the task of arousing bubbling laughter instead of consuming doubt.

The world has been better for him, and when that can be said of a man, the tears that drop upon his grave are more potent than the loud huzzas that follow the requiem of the greatest conqueror or the most successful statesman.

The kindliest thoughts and the sincerest prayers follow the great humanitarian—for such he was into the great beyond, and such solace as the hearty condolement of a million people can bring to the bereaved loved ones of Bill Nye, is theirs.

To a Portrait

She might have been some princess fair,
From Nile's banks where lotus blooms;
Or one of Pharaoh's daughters there
Asleep amid long molded tombs.

Or fairy princess sweet and proud,
Or gipsy queen with regal smiles;
Helen of Troy, or Guinevere,
Or Vivien with her witching smile.

Or Zozo's Queen, or Lily Clay,
Or Mrs. Langtry; or a maid
Of fashion, who, in costume scant,
Her charms is wont to have arrayed.

But none of these she is—not e'en,
Andromeda chained on the rocks.
I found her lovely, lone, and lorn
A chromo on a cracker box.

A Guarded Secret

It is time to call a halt upon the persistent spreaders of the alleged joke that a woman can not keep a secret. No baser ingratitude has been shown by man toward the fair sex than the promulgation of this false report. Whenever a would-be humorous man makes use of this antiquated chestnut which his fellow men feel in duty bound to applaud, the face of the woman takes on a strange, inscrutable, pitying smile that few men ever read.

The truth is that it is only woman who can keep a secret. Only a divine intelligence can understand the marvelous power with which ninety-nine married women out of a hundred successfully hide from the rest of the world the secret that they have bound themselves to something unworthy of the pure and sacrificing love they have given them. She may whisper to her neighbor that Mrs. Jones has turned her old silk dress twice, but if she has in her breast anything affecting one she loves, the gods themselves could not drag it from her.

Weak man looks into the wine cup and behold, he babbles his innermost thoughts to any gaping bystander; woman can babble of the weather, and gaze with infantine eyes into the orbs of the wiliest diplomat, while holding easily in her breast the heaviest secrets of state.

Adam was the original blab; the first telltale, and we are not proud of him. With the dreamy, appealing eyes of Eve upon him—she who was created for his comfort and pleasure—even as she stood by his side, loving and fresh and fair as a spring moon, the wretched cad said, "The woman gave me and I did eat." This reprehensible act in our distinguished forefather can not be excused by any gentleman who knows what is due to a lady.

Adam's conduct would have caused his name to be stricken from the list of every decent club in the country. And since that day, woman has stood by man, faithful, true, and ready to give up all for his sake. She hides his puny peccadilloes from the world, she glosses over his wretched misdemeanors, and she keeps silent when a word would pierce his inflated greatness and leave him a shriveled and shrunken rag.

And man says that woman can not keep a secret!

Let him be thankful that she can, or his littleness would be proclaimed from the housetops.

A Pastel

Above all hangs the dreadful night.

He pleads with her.

His hand is on her arm.

They stand in the cold, solemn night, gazing into a brilliantly lighted room. His face is white and terror-stricken. Hers is willful, defiant, and white with the surging impulse of destiny.

Ten miles away on the Harrisburg road a draggle-tailed rooster crows, but the woman does not falter.

He pleads with her.

She shakes off his hand with a gesture of loathing, and takes a step forward toward the lighted room.

He pleads with her.

Crystal flakes of moonlight quiver on the trees above; star dust flecks the illimitable rim of the Ineligible. The whicheverness of the Absolute reigns preeminent.

Sin is below; peace above.

The whip of the north wind trails a keen lash upon them. Carriages sweep by. Frost creeps upon the stones, lies crustily along parapets, spangles and throws back in arctic scintillation the moon's challenging rays.

He pleads with her.

At last she turns, conquered.

He has refused to treat to oysters.

Jim

Thanks, young man; I'll sit awhile,
And rest while Betsy trades a bit.
We've druv 'bout twenty mile to-day;
I'm real tired. Just think of it!

"Me a-restin' on this here bench
'Mongst all these trees and flowers and sich;
A park! You say? It's a nice place
To drive your team and stop and hitch.

"Farm? Yes, we've got a good one;
Two hundred acres as fine as you'll see,
We're purty well fixed as to worldly things,
We've worked hard for it, Betsy and me.

"But there's one thing keeps me mighty sad,
We can't get over it, night or day.
Never an hour we don't think of Jim—
Ten years now, since he went away.

"Dead?—No; just got mad and left.
Never a word have we heard from him;
Ten years of waitin', hopin', and prayin'
Jest fur one more sight of Jim.

"Jest about your height, young man;
Slender and straight as a stalk of corn;
Good as gold, though quick to get angry—
But, then he was mine and Betsy's first-born.

"I think if I could git hold of Jim's hand,
And kinder explain the words I said,
He'd know his old dad's heart would ever
Be just the same—but I guess Jim's dead.

"Or he never—what's that you say, sir?
You Jim!—My God!—it can't be true!
Come to my heart, boy—closer, closer—
Can it be Jim—oh, can it be you?

"Run quick and call your mother!
She's in the store—come quick again;
I'll wait here for you....

… Here! Police! Police!
That young feller's got my watch and chain!"

Board and Ancestors

The snake reporter of the Post was wending his way homeward last night when he was approached by a very gaunt, hungry-looking man with wild eyes and an emaciated face.

"Can you tell me, sir," he inquired, "where I can find in Houston a family of lowborn scrubs?"

"I don't exactly understand," said the reporter.

"Let me tell you how it is," said the emaciated man. "I came to Houston a month ago, and I hunted up a boarding house, as I can not afford to live at a hotel. I found a nice, aristocratic-looking place that suited me, and went inside. The landlady came in the parlor and she was a very stately lady with a Roman nose. I asked the price of board, and she said: 'Eighty dollars per month.' I fell against the door jamb with a dull thud, and she said:

"'You seem surprised, sah. You will please remember that I am the widow of Governah Riddle of Virginia. My family is very highly connected; give you board as a favah; I never consider money an equivalent to advantage of my society. Will you have a room with a door in it?'

"'I'll call again,' I said, and got out of the house, somehow, and went to another fine, three-storied house, with a sign 'Board and Rooms' on it.

"The next lady I saw had gray curls, and a soft gazelle-like eye. She was a cousin of General Mahone of Virginia and wanted $16 per week for a little back room with a pink motto and a picture of the battle of Chancellorsville in it.

"I went to some more boarding houses.

"The next lady said she was descended from Aaron Burr on one side and Captain Kidd on the other. She was using the Captain Kidd side in her business. She wanted to charge me sixty cents an hour for board and lodging. I traveled around all over Houston and found nine widows of Supreme Court judges, twelve relicts of governors and generals, and twenty-two ruins left by happy departed colonels, professors, and majors, who put fancy figures on the benefits of their society, and carried victuals as a side line.

"I finally grew desperately hungry and engaged a week's board at a nice, stylish mansion in the third ward. The lady who kept it was tall and imposing. She kept one hand lying across her waist and the other held a prayer book and a pair of ice hooks. She said she was an aunt of Davy Crockett, and was still in mourning for him. Her family was one of the first in Texas. It was then supper time and I went in to supper. Supper was from six-fifty to seven, and consisted of baker's bread, prayer, and cold slaw. I was so fatigued that I begged to be shown to my room immediately after the meal.

"I took the candle, went into the room she showed me, and locked the door quickly. The room was furnished in imitation of the Alamo. The walls and the floor were bare, and the bed was something like a monument only harder. About midnight I felt something as if I had fallen into a prickly pear bush, and jumped up and lit the candle. I looked in the bed and then put on my clothes, and exclaimed:

"'Thermopylae had her messenger of defeat, but the Alamo had a thousand.'

"I slipped out of the door and left the house.

"Now, my dear sir, I am not wealthy, and I can not afford to pay for high lineage and moldy ancestors with my board. Corned beef goes further with me than a coronet, and when I am cold a coat-of-arms does not warm me. I am desperate and hungry, and I hate everybody who can trace their ancestors farther back than the late Confederate Reunion. I want to find a boarding house whose proprietress was left while an infant in a basket at a livery stable, whose father was an unnaturalized dago from the fifth ward, and whose grandfather was never placed upon the map. I want to strike a low-down, scrubby, piebald, sans-culotte outfit that never heard of finger bowls or grace before meals but who can get up a mess of hot corn bread and Irish stew at regular market quotations. Is there any such place in Houston?"

The snake reporter shook his head sadly. "I never heard of any," he said. "The boarding houses here are run by ladies who do not take boarders to make a living; they are all trying to get a better rating in Bradstreet's than Hetty Green."

"Then," said the emaciated man desperately, "I will shake you for a long toddy."

The snake reporter felt in his vest pocket haughtily for a moment, and then refusing the proposition scornfully, moved away down the dimly lighted street.

An X-Ray Fable

And it came to pass that a man with a Cathode Ray went about the country finding out and showing the people, for a consideration, the insides of folks' heads and what they were thinking about. And he never made a mistake.

And in a certain town lived a man whose name was Reuben and a maid whose name was Ruth. And the two were sweethearts and were soon to be married.

And Reuben came to the man and hired him with coin to take a snap shot at Ruth's head, and find out whom she truly loved.

And later on Ruth came and also hired the man to find out whom Reuben truly loved. And the man did so and got two good negatives.

In the meantime Reuben and Ruth confessed to each other what they had done, and the next day they came together, hand in hand, to the man with the Ray, for their answer. The man saw them, and he wrote two names on two slips of paper and gave them into their hands.

"On these slips of paper," he said, "you will find the name of the one whom each of you loves best in the world, as truly discovered by my wonderful Cathode Ray."

And the man and the maid opened the pieces of paper and saw written on one "Reuben" and on the other "Ruth," and they were filled with joy and happiness, and went away with arms about each other's waists.

But the man with the Ray neglected to mention the fact that the photographs he had taken showed that Reuben's head was full of deep and abiding love for Reuben and Ruth's showed her to be passionately enamored of Ruth.

The moral is that the proprietor of the Ray probably knew his business.

A Universal Favorite

The most popular and best loved young lady in the United States is Miss Annie Williams of Philadelphia. Her picture is possessed by more men, and is more eagerly sought after than that of Lillian Russell, Mrs. Langtry, or any other famous beauty. There is more demand for her pictures than for the counterfeit presentments of all the famous men and women in the world combined. And yet she is a modest, charming, and rather retiring young lady, with a face less beautiful than of a clear and classic outline.

Miss Williams is soon to be married, but it is expected that the struggle for her pictures will go on as usual.

She is the lady the profile of whose face served as the model for the head of Liberty on our silver dollar.

Spring

A Dialect Poem
Oh, dinna ye fash y'r sel' hinny,
Varum kanst du nicht the thing see?
Don't always be kicking, me darlint;
Toujours le même chose will not be.

Tout le monde will grow brighter, ye spalpeen;
Und das zeit will get better, you bet;
Arrah! now will yez stop dot complainin'
Und a creat pig quick move on you get.

Ach, Gott! gina de monka a peanutte;
Und schmile some, for sweet spring is here,
Gott in himmel, carrambo das was sehr gut,
Kase its purty nigh time fur bock beer.

The Sporting Editor on Culture

"Is the literary editor in?"

The sporting editor looked up from the paper he was reading, and saw a vision of female loveliness about twenty years of age, with soft blue eyes, and a heavy mass of golden brown hair arranged in a coiffure of the latest and most becoming style.

"Nope," said the sporting editor, "you can bet your life he ain't in. He's out trying to get bail for having assaulted a man who wrote to the Letter Box to ask if ten men could build a house in twenty-seven and one-half days by working eight hours a day, how many buttons would be required for a coat of paint for same house. Did you call to see about a poem, or did you want him to sneak you some coupons for the bicycle contest?"

"Neither," said the young lady, with dignity. "I am the secretary of the Houston Young Ladies' Society of Ethical Culture, and I was appointed a committee to call upon the literary editor and consult him as to the best plan for the exercise of our various functions."

"Now, that's a good thing," said the sporting editor. "I don't seem to exactly catch on to 'ethical,' but if it's anything like physical culture you girls are going in for, you've trotted up to the right rack. I can tell you more about the proper way to exercise your functions in one minute than the literary editor can in an hour. He understands all about the identity of the wherefore and the origin of the pyramids, but he can't punch the bag, or give you any pointers how to increase your chest measurement. How long has your society been in training?"

"We organized last month," answered the lady, looking at the cheerful face of the reporter rather doubtfully.

"Well, now, how do you girls breathe—with your lungs or with your diaphragm?"

"Sir?"

"Oh, you'll have to start in right, and you've got to know how to breathe. The first thing is to keep your chest out, your shoulders back, and go through arm exercises for a few days. Then you can try something like this: Keep the upper part of the figure erect, and standing on one leg, try to—"

"Sir!" exclaimed the young lady severely, "you are presumptuous. I do not understand your obscure talk. Our society is not connected with a gymnasium. Our aim is the encouragement of social ethics."

"Oh," returned the sporting editor, in a disappointed tone, "you are on the society and pink tea racket. Sorry. That lets me out. Hoped you were going in for athletics. You could do it so well, too. Take my advice now, and try that little exercise every morning for a week. You'll be surprised to see how much it will benefit your muscles. As I said, just stand on one—"

Bang! went the door, and the blue-eyed young lady was gone.

"It's a pity," said the sporting editor, "that these girls don't pay some attention to self-culture without that—that ethical part."

A Question of Direction

"Do you mean to tell me," gasped the horrified gentleman from Boston, "that this man you speak of was shot and killed at a meeting of your debating society, and by the presiding officer himself, during the discussion of a question, simply because he arose and made a motion that was considered out of order?"

"He certainly was, sure," said the colonel. "This is simply awful," said the traveler. "I must make a note of this occurrence so that the people of my State can be apprised of the dreadful lawlessness that prevails in this section—a man shot down and killed at a social and educational meeting for the infringement of an unimportant parliamentary error! It is awful to contemplate."

"That's whatever," said the colonel reflectively. "It is for a fact. But you might state, in order to do justice to our community and town, which is, as it were, the Athens of Texas, that the motion made by the deceased was in the direction of his hip pocket. Shall we all liquor?"

The Old Farm

Just now when the whitening blossoms flare.
On the apple trees, and the growing grass
Creeps forth, and a balm is in the air;
With my lighted pipe and well-filled glass
Of the old farm I am dreaming,
And softly smiling, seeming
To see the bright sun beaming
Upon the old home farm.

And when I think how we milked the cows,
And hauled the hay from the meadows low,
And walked the furrows behind the plows,
And chapped the cotton to make it grow,
I'd much rather be here dreaming,
And, smiling, only seeming
To see that hot sun beaming
Upon the old home farm.

Willing to Compromise

As he walked up to the bar he pulled up his collar with both hands and straightened the old red tie that was trying to creep around under one ear.

The bartender glanced at him and then went on chipping lemon peel into a saucer.

"Say," said the man with the red tie, "it makes me right sick to think about it."

"What?" said the bartender, "water?"

"No sir; the apathy displayed by the people of the state in regard to presenting the battleship Texas with a suitable present. It is a disgrace to our patriotism. I was talking to W. G. Cleveland this morning and we both agreed that something must be done at once. Would you give ten dollars toward a silver service to be presented to the ship?"

The bartender reached behind him and took up a glass that was sitting on the shelf.

"I don't know that I would give you ten dollars," he said, "but here's some whisky that I put some turpentine in by mistake this morning and forgot to throw it out. Will that do as well?"

"It will," said the man with the red tie, reaching for the glass, "and I am also soliciting aid for the Cuban patriots. If you want to assist the cause of liberty and can't spare the cash, if you could rustle up a glass of beer with a fly in it, I would—"

"Trot out, now," said the bartender. "There's a church member looking in the back door, and he won't come in till everybody's out."

Ridiculous

The following conundrum was left at the office yesterday by a young man, who immediately fled:

"Why is the coming Sunday like a very young body?"

Answer: "Because it's neck's weak."

We do not see any reason why this should be the case. It is impossible for Sunday or any other day in the week to have a neck. The thing is printed merely to show what kind of stuff people send in to the paper.

Guessed Everything Else

A man with a long, sharp nose and a big bundle which he carried by a strap went up the steps of the gloomy-looking brick house, set his bundle down, rang the bell, and took off his hat and wiped his brow.

A woman opened the door and he said: "Madam, I have a number of not only useful but necessary articles here that I would like to show you. First, I want you to look at these elegant illustrated books of travel and biography, written by the best authors. They are sold only by subscription. They are bound in—"

"I don't care to see them. We have sm—"

"Small children only, eh? Well, Madam, here are some building blocks that are very instructive and amusing. No? Well, let me show you some beautiful lace window curtains for your sitting room, handmade and a great bargain. I can—"

"I don't want them. We have sm—"

"Smoking in the house? It won't injure them in the least. Just shake them out in the morning and I guarantee not a vestige of tobacco smoke will remain. Here also I have a very ingenious bell for awakening lazy servants in the morning. You simply touch a button and—"

"I tell you we have sm—"

"Have smart servants, have you? Well, that is a blessing. Now, here is a clothes line that is one of the wonders of the age. It needs no pins and can be fastened to anything—fence, side of the house, or tree. It can be raised or lowered in an instant, and for a large washing is the most convenient and laborsaving invention that—"

"I say we have small—"

"Oh, you have a small family. Let's see, then I have here a—"

"I'm trying to tell you," said the woman, "that we have smallpox in the family, and—"

The long-nosed man made a convulsive grab at his goods and rolled down the steps in about two seconds, while the woman softly closed the door just as a man got out of a buggy and nailed a yellow flag on the house.

The Prisoner of Zembla

By Anthony Hoke

So the king fell into a furious rage, so that none durst go near him for fear, and he gave out that since the Princess Astla had disobeyed him there would be a great tourney, and to the knight who should prove himself of the greatest valor he would give the hand of the princess.

And he sent forth a herald to proclaim that he would do this.

And the herald went about the country making his desire known, blowing a great tin horn and riding a noble steed that pranced and gamboled; and the villagers gazed upon him with awe and said: "Lo, that is one of them tin horn gamblers concerning which the chroniclers have told us."

And when the day came, the king sat in the grandstand, holding the gage of battle in his hand, and by his side sat the Princess Astla, looking very pale and beautiful, but with mournful eyes from which she scarce could keep the tears, and the knights who came to the tourney gazed upon the princess in wonder at her beauty, and each swore to win her so that he could marry her and board with the king. Suddenly the heart of the princess gave a great bound, for she saw among the knights one of the poor students with whom she had been in love.

The knights mounted and rode in a line past the grandstand, and the king stopped the poor student, who had the worst horse and the poorest caparisons of any of the knights, and said:

"Sir knight, prithee tell me of what that marvelous shaky and rusty-looking armor of thine is made?"

"Oh, king," said the young knight, "seeing that we are about to engage in a big fight, I would call it scrap iron, wouldn't you?"

"Ods bodikins!" said the king. "The youth hath a pretty wit."

The tourney lasted the whole day and at the end but two of the knights were left, one of them being the princess's lover.

"Here's enough for a fight, anyhow," said the king. "Come hither, oh knights, will ye joust for the hand of this lady fair?"

"We joust will," said the knights.

The two knights fought for two hours and at length the princess's lover prevailed and stretched the other upon the ground. The victorious knight made his horse caracole before the king, and bowed low in his saddle.

On the Princess Astla's cheek was a rosy flush; in her eyes the light of excitement vied with the soft glow of love; her lips were parted, her lovely hair unbound, and she grasped the arms of her chair and leaned forward with heaving bosom and happy smile to hear the words of her lover.

"You have fought well, sir knight," said the king. "And if there is any boon you crave you have but to name it."

"Then," said the knight, "I will ask you this: I have bought the patent rights in your kingdom for Schneider's celebrated monkey wrench and I want a letter from you endorsing it."

"You shall have it," said the king, "but I must tell you that there is not a monkey in my kingdom."

With a yell of rage the victorious knight threw himself on his horse and rode away at a furious gallop.

The king was about to speak when a horrible suspicion flashed upon him and he fell dead upon the grandstand.

"My God!" he cried, as he expired, "he has forgotten to take the princess with him."

Lucky Either Way

The Memphis Commercial-Appeal, in commenting on errors in grammar made by magazines, takes exception to an error in construction occurring in Gode's Magazine in which, in J. H. Connelly's story entitled "Mr. Pettigrew's Bad Dog," a character is made to say: "You will be lucky if you escape with only marrying one."

A man says this to another one who is being besieged by two ladies, and the Commercial-Appeal thinks he intended to say: "You will be lucky if you escape with marrying only one."

Now, after considering the question, it seems likely that there is more in Mr. J. H. Connelly's remark than is dreamed of in the philosophy of the Commercial-Appeal.

The history of matrimony gives color to the belief that, to whichever one of the ladies the gentleman might unite himself, he would be lucky if he escaped with only marrying her. Getting married is the easiest part of the affair. It is what comes afterward that makes a man sometimes wish a wolf had carried him into the forest when he was a little boy. It takes only a little nerve, a black coat, from five to ten dollars, and a girl, for a man to get married. Very few men are lucky enough to escape with only marrying a woman. Women are sometimes so capricious and unreasonable that they demand that a man stay around afterward, and board and clothe them, and build fires, and chop wood, and rock the chickens out of the garden, and tell the dressmaker when to send in her bill again.

We would like to read "Mr. Pettigrew's Bad Dog" and find out whether the man was lucky enough to only marry the lady, or whether she held on to him afterward and didn't let him escape.

The "Bad Man"

A bold, bad man made a general display of himself in a Texas town a few days ago. It seems that he'd imbibed a sufficient number of drinks to become anxious to impress the town with his badness, and when the officers tried to arrest him he backed up against the side of a building and defied arrest. A considerable crowd of citizens, among whom were a number of drummers from a hotel close by, had gathered to witness the scene.

The bad man was a big, ferocious-looking fellow with long, curling hair that fell on his shoulders, a broad-brimmed hat, a buckskin coat with fringe around the bottom, and a picturesque vocabulary. He was flourishing a big six-shooter and swore by the bones of Davy Crockett that he would perforate the man who attempted to capture him.

The city marshal stood in the middle of the street and tried to reason with him, but the bad man gave a whoop and rose up on his toes, and the whole crowd fell back to the other side of the street. The police had a conference, but none of them would volunteer to lead the attack.

Presently a little, wizened, consumptive-looking drummer for a Connecticut shoe factory squeezed his way through the crowd on the opposite side of the street to have a peep at the desperado. He weighed about ninety pounds and wore double glass spectacles. Just then the desperado gave another whoop and yelled:

"Gol darn ye, why don't some of ye come and take me? I'll eat any five of ye without chawin', and I ain't hungry either—whoopee!"

The crowd fell back a few yards further and the police turned pale again, but the skinny little man adjusted his spectacles with both hands, and stepped on to the edge of the sidewalk and took a good look at the bad men. Then he deliberately struck across the street at a funny hopping kind of a run right up to where the terror stood.

The crowd yelled at him to come back, and the desperado flourished his six-shooter again, but the little man went straight up to him and said something. The crowd shuddered and expected to see him fall with a forty-five bullet in him, but he didn't. They saw the desperado lower his pistol and run his hand in his pocket and hand something to the little man.

Then the desperado walked sheepishly down the sidewalk, and the little man came back across the street.

"Bad man?" he said. "I guess not. He wouldn't hurt a fly. That's Zeke Skinner. He was raised on the farm next to me in Connecticut. He's selling some kind of fake liver medicine, and that's his street rig he's got on now. I loaned him eight dollars in Hartford nine years ago, and never expected to see him again. Thought I knew his voice. Pay? I reckon he paid me. I calculate I always collect what's owing to me."

Then the crowd scattered and the twelve policeman headed Zeke off at the next corner and clubbed him all the way to the station house.

A Slight Mistake

An ordinary-looking man wearing a last season's negligee shirt stepped into the business office and unrolled a strip of manuscript some three feet long.

"I wanted to see you about this little thing I want to publish in the paper. There are fifteen verses besides the other reading matter. The verses are on spring. My handwriting is a trifle illegible and I may have to read it over to you. This is the way it runs:

> Spring
>
> "The air is full of gentle zephyrs,
> Grass is growing green;
> Winter now has surely left us.
> Spring has come, I ween.
>
> "When the sun has set, the vapors
> Rise from out the meadows low;
> When the stars are lit like tapers
> Then the night winds chilly blow."

"Take that stuff up to the editorial department," said the business manager shortly.

"I have been up there already," said the ordinary-looking man, "and they sent me down here. This will fill about a column. I want to talk with you about the price. The last verse runs this way:

> "Then it is that weakening languors
> Thicken in our veins the blood
> And we must ward off these dangers
> Ere we find our names are 'Mud.'"

"The reading matter that follows is, as you see, typewritten, and easily read. Now, I—"

"D——n it," said the business manager. "Don't you come in here reading your old spring poems to me. I've been bored already today with a lot of ink and paper drummers. Why don't you go to work instead of fooling away your time on rot like that?"

"I didn't mean to bother you," said the other man, rolling up his manuscript. "Is there another paper in the city?"

"Yes, there's a few. Have you got a family?"

"Yes, sir."

"Then why in thunder don't you get into some decent business, instead of going around writing confounded trash and reading it to busy people? Ain't you got any manhood about you?"

"Excuse me for troubling you," said the ordinary-looking man, as he walked toward the door. "I tell you how it is. I cleared over $80,000 last year on these little things I write. I am placing my spring and summer ads for the Sarsaparilla firm of which I am a member. I had decided to place about $1,000 in advertising in this town. I will see the other papers you spoke of. Good morning!"

The business manager has since become so cautious that all the amateur poets in the city now practice reading their verses to him, and he listens without a murmur.

Delayed

There's a good time coming—so the optimists all say;
When everything will be alive and humming.
And we'll have lots of money and sing and dance all day;
It may be so—but it's a good time coming.

A Good Story Spoiled

Few nights ago in a rather tough saloon in a little town on the Central Railroad, a big, strapping desperado, who had an unenviable reputation as a bad man generally, walked up to the bar and in a loud voice ordered everybody in the saloon to walk up and take a drink. The crowd moved quickly to the bar at his invitation, as the man was half drunk and was undoubtedly dangerous when in that condition.

One man alone failed to accept the invitation. He was a rather small man, neatly dressed, who sat calmly in his chair, gazing idly at the crowd. A student of physiognomy would have been attracted by the expression of his face, which was one of cool determination and force of will. His jaw was square and firm, and his eye gray and steady, with that peculiar gray glint in the iris that presages more danger than any other kind of optic.

The bully looked around and saw that someone had declined his invitation.

He repeated it in a louder voice.

The small man rose to his feet and walked coolly toward the desperado.

"Excuse me," he said in a low but determined tone, "I'm a little deaf and didn't hear you the first time. Gimme whisky straight."

And another story was spoiled for the papers.

Revenge

> *The man, woman, child, or animal who pens "Postscripts" for the Houston Post is a weird, wild-eyed genius and ought to be captured and put on exhibition with the "nameless things" they are taking out of the government well at San Marcos. There is certainly a reward for both specimens.*
>
> Kyle Star-Vindicator

Although we can stand a great deal, this attack has goaded us to what is perhaps a bitter and cruel, but not entirely an unjustifiable revenge. Below will be found an editorial from the last number of the Star-Vindicator:

"Spring, with her magic word of music, pathos, and joy, has touched a thousand hills and vales, has set a million throats to warbling; sunshine, song, and flowers bedeck every altar and crown each day more glorious. Imperial spring is here—the brightest, gayest, and best of all God's seasons.

Springtime is like the little child—crowned with its own purity and love not tarnished and seared with the hand of Time. It is like the bright, sparkling miniature rivulet that bursts from the mountain side and goes merrily over the shining pebbles before it hastens into a dark, deep, dangerous river. The sweet cadence of music, the scent of wafted perfumes, the stretch of glorious landscape, radiated and beautified with lovely gems of Oriental hue, catch our attention at every step. The world today is a wilderness of flowers, a bower of beauty, and millions of sweet native warblers make its pastures concert halls, where we can go in peace at even-time, after the strife, the toil, the disappointments, and sorrows of our labors here and gather strength, courage, and hope to meet on the morrow life's renewed duties and responsibilities."

No Help for It

"John," said a Houston grocer the other day to one of his clerks. "You have been a faithful and competent clerk, and in order to show my appreciation, I have decided to take you into partnership. From this time on you are to have a share in the business, and be a member of the firm."

"But, sir," said John anxiously, "I have a family to support. I appreciate the honor, but I fear I am too young for the responsibility. I would much rather retain my present place."

"Can't help it," said the grocer. "Times are hard and I've got to cut down expenses if I have to take every clerk in the house into the firm."

Rileys Luck

Riley was a lazy fellow,
Never worked a bit;
All day long in some store corner
On a chair he'd sit.

Never talked much—too much trouble—
Tired his jaws, you see;
When his folks got out of victuals,
"Just my luck!" says he.

Fellow offered him ten dollars
If he'd work two days;
Riley crossed his legs and looked up
Through the sun's hot rays;

Then he leaned back in the shadow,
Sadly shook his head;
"Never asked me till hot weather—
Just my luck!" he said.

Riley courted Sally Hopkins
In a quiet way;
When he saw Jim Dobsen kiss her,
"Just my luck!" he'd say.

Leap Year came, and Mandy Perkins
Sought his company;
Riley sighed, and married Mandy—
"Just my luck!" he'd say.

Riley took his wife out fishing
In a little boat;
Storm blew up and turned them over;
Mandy couldn't float.

Riley sprang into the river,
Seized her by the hair.
Swam a mile into the shore where
Friends pulled out the pair.

Mandy was so full of water
Seemed she'd surely die.
Doctors worked with her two hours
Ere she moved an eye.

They told Riley she was better;
Doctors were in glee.
Riley chewed an old pine splinter—
"Just my luck!" says he.

“Not So Much a Tam Fool”

A man without a collar, wearing a white vest and holes in his elbows, walked briskly into a Congress Street grocery last Saturday with a package in his hand and said:

“Here, Fritz, I bought two dozen eggs here this afternoon, and I find your clerk made a mistake, I—”

“Coom here, Emil,” shouted the grocer, “you hof dis shentleman sheated mit dos rotten eggs. Gif him ein dozen more, und—”

“But you don’t understand me,” said the man, with a pleasant smile. “The mistake is the other way. The eggs are all right; but you have given me too many. I only paid for two dozen, and on reaching home I find three dozen in the sack. I want to return the extra dozen, and I came back at once. I—”

“Emil!” shouted the grocer again to his boy. “Gif dis man two dozen eggs at vonce. You haf sheated him mit pad eggs. Don’d you do dot any more times or I discharge you.”

“But, sir,” said the man with the white vest, anxiously. “You gave me too many eggs for my money, and I want to return a dozen. I am too honest to—”

“Emil,” said the grocer, “gif dis man t’ree dozen goot fresh eggs at vonce and let him go. Ve makes pad eggs good ven ve sells dem. Hurry up quick and put in drei or four extra vons.”

“But, listen to me, sir,” said the man. “I want to—”

“Say, mein frindt,” said the grocer in a lower voice, “you petter dake dose eggs und go home. I know vat you pring pack dose eggs for. If I dake dem, I say, ‘Veil, dot is ein very good man; he vas honest py dose eggs, aind’t it?’ Den you coom pack Monday und you puy nine tollers’ vorth of vlour and paeon and canned goots, and you say you bay me Saturday night. I was not so much a tarn fool as eferypody say I look like. You petter dake dose t’ree dozen eggs and call it skvare. Ve always correct leedle misdakes ven ve make dem. Emil, you petter make it t’ree dozen und a half fur good measure, and put in two t’ree stick candy for die kinder.”

A Guess-Proof Mystery Story

The most popular and recent advertising dodge in literature is the Grand Guess Contest Mystery Story. Everybody is invited to guess how the story will end, at any time before the last chapter is published, and incidentally to buy a paper or subscribe. It is the easiest thing in the world to write a story of mystery that will defy the most ingenious guessers in the country.

To prove it, here is one that we offer $10,000 to any man and $15,000 to any woman who guesses the mystery before the last chapter.

The synopsis of the story is alone given, as literary style is not our object—we want mystery.

Chapter I

Judge Smith, a highly esteemed citizen of Plunkville, is found murdered in his bed at his home. He has been stabbed with a pair of scissors, poisoned with "rough on rats." His throat has been cut with an ivory handled razor, an artery in his arm has been opened, and he has been shot full of buckshot from a double-barreled gun.

The coroner is summoned and the room examined. On the ceiling is a bloody footprint, and on the floor are found a lady's lace handkerchief, embroidered with the initials "J. B.," a package of cigarettes and a ham sandwich. The coroner renders a verdict of suicide.

Chapter II

The judge leaves a daughter, Mabel, aged eighteen, and ravishingly lovely. The night before the murder she exhibited a revolver and an axe in the principal saloon in town and declared her intention of "doing up" the old man. The judge has his life insured for $100,000 in her favor. Nobody suspects her of the crime.

Mabel is engaged to a young man named Charlie, who is seen on the night of the murder by several citizens climbing out the judge's window with a bloody razor and a shotgun in his hand. Society gives Charlie the cold shoulder.

A tramp is run over by a street car and before dying confesses to having committed the murder, and at the judge's funeral his brother, Colonel Smith, breaks down and acknowledges having killed the judge in order to get his watch. Mabel sends to Chicago and employs a skilled detective to work up the case.

Chapter III

A beautiful strange lady dressed in mourning comes to Plunkville and registers at the hotel as Jane Bumgartner. (The initials on the handkerchief!)

The next day a Chinaman is found who denies having killed the judge, and is arrested by the detective. The strange lady meets Charlie on the street, and, on smelling the smoke from his cigarette, faints. Mabel discards him and engages herself to the Chinaman.

Chapter IV

While the Chinaman is being tried for murder, Jane Bumgartner testifies that she saw the detective murder Judge Smith at the instance of the minister who conducted the funeral, and that Mabel is Charlie's stepmother. The Chinaman is about to confess when footsteps are heard approaching. The next chapter will be the last, and it is safe to say that no one will find it easy to guess the ending of the story. To show how difficult this feat is, the last chapter is now given.

Chapter V

The footsteps prove to be those of Thomas R. Hefflebomer of Washington Territory, who introduces positive proof of having murdered the judge during a fit of mental aberration, and Mabel marries a man named Tompkins, whom she met two years later at Hot Springs.

Futility

To be so near—and then to vanish
Like some unreal creature of the sense;
To come so near that every fiber, tingling,
Makes ready welcome; then to surge
Back into the recesses of the strange,
Mysterious unknown. Ye gods!
What agony to feel thee slowly steal
Away from us when, with caught breath
And streaming eyes, and parted lips,
We fain would with convulsive gasp
And tortured features bow our frame
In one loud spasm of homage to thy spell!
But with what grief we find we can not do it;
The dream is o'er—we can not sneeze.

The Wounded Veteran

A party of Northern tourists passed through Houston the other day, and while their train was waiting at the depot an old colored man, with one arm bandaged and hung in an old red handkerchief for a sling, walked along the platform.

"What's the matter with your arm, uncle?" called out one of the tourists.

"It was hurt in de wah, sah. Hab you any 'bacco you could gib a po' ole niggah, sah?"

Several of the tourists poked their heads out of the car windows to listen, and in a few moments the old darky had taken up a collection in his hat, consisting of a plug of tobacco, three or four cigars, and sundry nickels, dimes, and quarters.

"How were you wounded?" asked a tourist. "Were you shot in the arm?"

"No, sah; hit wusn't exac' by a shot."

"Piece of shell strike you?"

"No, sah; wusn't a shell."

"Bayonet wound, maybe?"

"No, boss, hit wusn't a bayonet."

"What battle were you in?"

"Do' know ef it had a name, but hit was a mighty hot fight while it lasted."

"Do you draw a pension?"

"No, boss."

"It seems it would be a charitable act," said a tourist to the others, "to take this old darky's name and see that he gets the pension he is certainly entitled to. What is your name, uncle?"

"Mose Atkisson, sah."

"Now, Mose," said the tourist, "give me the particulars of the engagement you were in, and the date, and all the information you possess about the manner in which you were wounded, and the government will pay you a nice little sum every three months to help you along."

"Am dat so, boss?" asked the old darky, his eyes growing big with wonder. "Den I'll sho tell you about hit. Hit wus jes' befor' supper en I was totin' a big chance ob wood in to make a fiah, when—"

"Never mind about what you did in camp," said the tourist. "Tell us in which battle of the War of the Rebellion were you engaged."

"It wusn't dat wah, boss; it wus de wah wid Spain."

"What do you mean?"

"Lemme tell you how it wus. I cuts wood and does odd jobs up to Cunnel Wadkinses. Cunnel Wadkins am de bigges' fighter in de Souf. W'en dis here wah wid Spain cum up in de papers Cunnel Wadkins 'low he gwine ter pulverize de whole Spanish nation. He set all day in de saloon an' he talk about it, an' he cum home at meal time an' he git out his ole' s'ord, an' he don' talk about nuthin' else.

"Mis' Susie, de Cunnel's wife, she suppote de family, an' she do de cookin'. Las' Sadday night de Cunnel cum home, an' he been drinkin' plenty. Mis' Susie she look at him an' shet her mouf tight, an' say nothin'.

"De Cunnel git out de s'ord an' 'low dat de day ob recknin' am cum wid de cruel an' bloodthusty Spaniards. Mis' Susie went on fryin' batter cakes, but Land! don't I know dat woman gwine ter bus' things wide open putty soon!

"I fetch in a turn ob wood; de Cunnel he settin' by de kitchen stobe, kinder rockin' roun' in de chur. Es I cum in de do' Cunnel say: 'You is treat me col', Madam, kase I uphol' de dignity ob de Wadkins fambly. De Wadkinses nebber wuk; dey am solgers an' am got ter keep ready fur der country's call.'

"'Treats you col', does I?' says Mis' Susie. 'Well, den, lemme treat you warm some,' says she.

"She po' out of de bilin' tea-kittle a big pan full ob hot water an' she fling it all ober de Cunnel. I gits a big lot ob it on dis arm as I was pilin' de wood in de box, an' it tuk de skin off, an' I dun had it wrapped up fo' days. De Cunnel am in bed yit, but he sw'ar w'en he git up he gwine ter wuk.

"Dat's how dis here wah wid Spain done up dis ole niggah. 'Bout w'en, boss, will de fus' payment ob dat penshun git here, do you recum?"

"The ignorance and stupidity," said the tourist, as he shut down his window, "of the colored man in the South are appalling."

Her Ruse

"How do I keep John home of nights?" asked a Houston lady of a friend the other day.

"Well, I struck a plan once by a sudden inspiration, and it worked very nicely. John had been in a habit of going downtown every night after supper and staying until ten or eleven o'clock. One night he left as usual, and after going three or four blocks he found he had forgotten his umbrella and came back for it. I was in the sitting room reading, and he slipped in the room on his tiptoes and came up behind me and put his hands over my eyes. John expected me to be very much startled, I suppose, but I only said softly, 'Is that you, Tom?' John hasn't been downtown at night since."

Why Conductors Are Morose

Street car conductors often have their tempers tried by the inconsiderate portion of the public, but they are not allowed to ease their feelings by "talking back." One of them related yesterday an occurrence on his line a few days ago.

A very fashionably dressed lady, accompanied by a little boy, was in the car, which was quite full of people. "Conductor," she said languidly, "let me know when we arrive at Peas Avenue."

When the car arrived at that street the conductor rang the bell and the car stopped.

"Peas Avenue, ma'am," he said, climbing off to assist her from the car.

The lady raised the little boy to his knees and pointed out the window at the name of the street which was on a board, nailed to the corner of a fence.

"Look, Freddy," she said, "that tall, straight letter with a funny little curl at the top is a '*P*.' Now don't forget it again. You can go on, conductor; we get off at Gray Street."

"Only to Lie—"

Only to lie in the evening,
Watching the drifting clouds,
O'er the blue heavens sailing;
Mystical, dreamlike shrouds.
Watching the purple shadows
Filling the woodland glades,
Only to lie in the twilight
Deep in the gathering shade.

Only to lie at midnight,
Climbing the pitch-dark stairs;
Wife at the top of them waiting;
Upwards are rising our hairs.
Only to lie as she asks us—
"Where have you been so late?"
Only to lie with judgment—
"Cars blocked; I had to wait."

The Pewee

In the hush of the drowsy afternoon.
When the very mind on the breast of June
Lies settled, and hot white tracery
Of the shattered sunlight flitters free
Through the unstinted leaves to the pied cool sward,
On a dead tree branch sings the saddest bard
Of the birds that be.
'Tis the lone pewee;
Its note is a sob, and its song is pitched
In a single key like a soul bewitched
To a mournful minstrelsy.

"Pewee, Pewee," doth it ever cry;
A sad, sweet, minor threnody
That threads the aisles of the dim hot grove
Like a tale of a wrong or a vanished love,
And the fancy comes that the wee dun bird
Perchance was a maid, and her heart was stirred
By some lover's rhyme
In a golden time,
And broke when the world turned false and old;
And her dreams grew dark and her faith grew cold,
In some fairy far-off clime.
And her soul crept into the pewee's breast;
And forever she cries with a strange unrest
For something lost, in the afternoon;
For something missed from the lavish June;
For the heart, that died in the long ago;
For the livelong pain that pierceth so;
Thus the pewee cries,
While the evening lies
Steeped in the languorous still sunshine,
Rapt, to the leaf and the bough and the vine,
Of some hopeless paradise.

The Sunday Excursionist

Somebody—who it was doesn't make any difference—has said something like the following: "There is something grand in the grief of the Common People, but there is no sadder sight on earth than that of a Philistine enjoying himself."

If a man would realize the truth of this, let him go on a Sunday excursion. The male Sunday excursionist enjoys himself, as the darkies say, "a gwine and a cornin'." No other being on earth can hold quite so much bubbling and vociferous joy. The welkin that would not ring when the Sunday excursionist opens his escape valve is not worth a cent. Six days the Sunday excursionist labors and does his work, but he does his best to refute the opponents of the theory of the late Charles Darwin. He occupies all the vacant seats in the car with his accomplices, and lets his accursed good nature spray over the rest of the passengers. He is so infernally happy that he wants everybody, to the brakeman on the rear car, to know it. He is so devilish agreeable, so perniciously jolly and so abominably entertaining that people who were bom with or have acquired brains love him most vindictively.

People who become enamored of the Sunday excursionist are apt to grow insanely jealous, and have been known to rise up and murder him when a stranger enters the car and he proceeds to repeat his funny remarks for the benefit of a fresh audience.

The female Sunday excursionist generally accompanies him. She brings her laugh with her, and does a turn in the pauses of his low comedy work. She never by any accident misplaces her laugh or allows it to get out of curl. It ripples naturally and conforms readily to the size of the car. She puts on the male Sunday excursionist's hat, and he puts on hers, and if the other passengers are feeling worse than usual, they sing "The Swanee River." There is enough woe and sorrow in the world without augmenting it in this way.

Men who have braved the deepest troubles and emerged unscathed from the heaviest afflictions have gone down with a shriek of horror and despair before the fatal hilarity of the Sunday excursionist. There is no escape from his effects.

Decoration Day

Decoration Day has passed, and the graves of the Northern and Southern soldiers have been duly flower strewn, as is meet and fitting. The valor of the North has been told on a thousand rostrums, and the courage of the South has been related from ten hundred platforms. Battles have been fought again, and redoubts retaken. Much has been said of brotherly love and the bridging of the chasm. The Blue has marched abreast to the common meeting place, and the Gray has marched abreast, and they have met and shaken hands and said the war is over. There can be no such thing as a union of the Blue and the Gray. When you pronounce the words you form the bar that separates them. The Blue is one thing and the Gray is another. There should be no more Blue and no more Gray. If a tribute is to be paid to the heroes on either side whom we wish to keep in remembrance, it should be made by American citizens, not divided by the colors of their garments. There is no need to march by grand armies, by camps, or by posts. If there is to be a shaking of hands, let it be by one citizen of the United States with another. The Gray and Blue are things of the past. In the innermost hearts, in the still, quick memories of the South, the Gray will always live, but it should live as in a shrine, hallowed and hidden from pomp and display. As citizens of a common country, we of the South offer our hands to citizens of the North in peace and fellowship, but we do not mingle the Gray with the Blue.

Charge of the White Brigade

Mehitabel, Claribel, Bessie, and Sue
All in white lawn and ribbons pale blue.
Went into a drug store; each sat on a stool,
And called for some phosphate to make them all cool.
"Oh! what is that big copper thing over there?"
Asked Bessie the gay one, asked Bessie the fair.
"Why that," said the clerk, "is the thing with which we
Charge the phosphate and soda we sell, don't you see?"
"How nice," said bright Bessie and then they all rose,
And shook out their ruffles and beautiful clothes;
"Please charge those we had," said the girls—then they flew,
Mehitabel, Claribel, Bessie, and Sue.

An Inspiration

He was seated on an empty box on Main Street late yesterday evening during the cold drizzling rain. He was poorly clad and his thick coat was buttoned up high under his chin. He had a woeful, harassed appearance, and there was something about him that indicated that he was different from the average tramp who beats his way by lies and fraud.

The *Post* man felt a touch of sympathy and went up to him and said:

"There's a place around the corner where you can get a lunch and lodging for a small sum. When did you strike town?"

The man gazed at the reporter out of his small, keen eyes and said:

"You're a new man on the *Post*, are you not?"

"Yes, comparatively."

"Do you see that block of three-story buildings over there?"

"Yes."

"Well, I own them and was just sitting here studying what I'm going to do."

"What's the trouble?"

"Why, the walls are cracking and bulging out on the sides, and I'm afraid I'm going to have to put a lot of money into repairs. I've got over one hundred tenants in those buildings."

"I'll tell you what to do."

"What?"

"You say the walls are bulging out?"

"Yes."

"Well, that makes more room everywhere. You just raise all your tenants' rent on account of the extra space."

"Young man, you're a genius. I'll put rents up twenty percent tomorrow."

And one more capitalist was saved.

Coming to Him

The man who keeps up with the latest scientific discoveries is abroad in the land. He knows all about bacilli, microbes, and all the various newly found foes to mankind. He reads the papers and heeds all the warnings that lead to longevity and safety to mind and limb. He stopped a friend on Main Street yesterday who was hurrying to the post-office and said excitedly:

"Wait a minute, Brown. Do you ever bite your finger nails?"

"I think so—no, I don't know; excuse me, please, I've got to catch that car."

"Hold on, man; great goodness alive, you don't know what danger you are in. If a sharp particle of the nail gets into your lungs, inflammation is bound to set in, and finally laceration, consumption, hemorrhage, fits, coma, tuberculosis, and death. Think of it! And by the way, a new bacillus has been found in water in which roses have been left standing that is very fatal. I want to warn you. Do you know that—"

"Say, old man, I'm much obliged, but this letter—"

"What is a letter compared with your life? There are 10,000,000 animalcules in a spoonful of ordinary hydrant water; there are 2,000 different varieties known. Do you ever put salt in your beer?"

"I don't know; I really must go, I—"

"Don't hold me responsible for your life, I'm trying to save it. Why, Heavens, man, it's nothing but a miracle that we live a single day. In every glass of beer there is an infinitesimal quantity of hydrochloric acid. Salt is a chloride of sodium, and the union releases the chlorine. You are drinking chlorine gas every day of your life. Pause, before it is too late."

"I don't drink beer."

"But you breathe through your mouth when you are asleep. Do you know what that does? Brings on angina pectoris and bronchitis. Are you determined to let your ignorance carry you to your grave? Think of your wife and children! Do you know that the common house fly carries 40,000 microbes on his feet, and can convey cholera, typhoid fever, diphtheria, pyaemia, and—"

"Dang your microbes. I've got just three minutes to catch that mail. So long."

"Wait just a minute. Dr. Pasteur says that—"

But the victim was gone.

Ten minutes later the heeder of new discoveries was knocked down by a wagon while trying to cross the street reading about a new filter, and was carried home by sympathizing friends.

His Pension

"Speaking of the $140,000,000 paid out yearly by the government in pensions," said a prominent member of Hood's brigade to the Post's representative, "I am told that a man in Indiana applied for a pension last month on account of a surgical operation he had performed on him during the war. And what do you suppose that surgical operation was?"

"Haven't the least idea."

"He had his retreat cut off at the battle of Gettysburg!"

The Winner

After the performance of "In Old Kentucky" Friday night three old cronies went into a saloon with the inflexible determination of taking a drink. After doing so, they added an amendment in the shape of another and then tacked on an emergency clause.

When they got to feeling a little mellow they sat down at a table and commenced lying. Not maliciously, but just ordinary, friendly lying, about the things they had seen and done. They all tried their hand at relating experiences, and as the sky was clear, there was no matinee performance of the Ananias tragedy.

Finally the judge suggested the concoction of a fine large julep—a julep that would render the use of curling irons unnecessary—and the one who told the most improbable story should be allowed to produce the vacuum in the straws.

The major and the judge led off with a couple of marvelous narratives which were about a tie. The colonel moistened his lips as his eye rested on the big glass filled with diamonds and amber, and crowned with fragrant mint. He commenced his story:

"The incident I am about to relate is not only wonderful, but true. It happened in this very town on Saturday afternoon. I got up rather early Saturday morning, as I had a big day's work ahead of me. My wife fixed me up a rattling good cocktail when I got up and I was feeling pretty good. When I came downstairs she handed me a five-dollar bill that had dropped out of my pocket and said: 'John, you must really get a better looking housemaid. Jane is so homely, and you never did admire her. See if you can find a real nice-looking one—and John, dear, you are working too hard. You must really have some recreation. Why not take Miss Muggins, your typewriter, out for a drive this afternoon? Then you might stop at the milliner's and tell them not to send up that hat I ordered, and—"

"Hold on. Colonel," said the judge. "You just drink that mint julep right now. You needn't go any further with your story."

Hungry Henry's Ruse

Hungry Henry: Madam, I am state agent for a new roller-action, unbreakable, double-elastic suspender. Can I show you some?

Mrs. Lonestreet: No, there ain't no man on the place.

Hungry Henry: Well, then, I am also handling something unique in the way of a silvermounted, morocco leather, dog collar, with name engraved free of charge. Perhaps—

Mrs. Lonestreet: 'Tain't no use. I ain't got a dog.

Hungry Henry: Hat's what I wanted to know. Now fix me de best supper you'se kin, and do it quick or it won't be healthy fur you. See?

A Proof of Love

"If you love me as I love you"—
(Ah, sweet those words to lover's ear,
'Twas Lois spake, in accents true,
So loving, tender, kind and dear.)

"If you love me as I love you"—
(Ah, heaven and earth were wrapped in bliss,
The wild rose listened, dissolved in dew;
The very zephyrs sought her kiss.)

"If you love me as I love you"—
(Ah, strains from Paradise her words!)
"And if I do, what then?" I asked;
While round us winged the listening birds.

"If you love me as I love you—"
She raised those fringèd eyes of jet,
And whispered low in pleading tones:
"Just fill the wood box, will you, pet?"

One Consolation

Breakfast was over and Adam had gone to his daily occupation of pasting the names of the animals on their cages. Eve took the parrot to one side and said: "It was this way. He made a big kick about those biscuits not being good at breakfast."

"And what did you say?" asked the parrot.

"I told him there was one consolation; he couldn't say his mother ever made any better ones."

An Unsuccessful Experiment

There is an old colored preacher in Texas who is a great admirer of the Rev. Sam Jones.[1] Last Sunday he determined to drop his old style of exhorting the brethren, and pitch hot shot plump into the middle of their camp, after the manner so successfully followed by the famous Georgia evangelist. After the opening hymn had been sung, and the congregation led in prayer by a worthy deacon, the old preacher laid his spectacles on his Bible, and let out straight from the shoulder.

"My dearly belubbed," he said, "I has been preachin' to you fo' mo' dan five years, and de grace ob God hab failed to percolate in yo' obstreperous hearts. I hab nebber seen a more or'nery lot dan dis belubbed congregation. Now dar is Sam Wadkins in de fo'th bench on de left. Kin anybody show me a no'counter, trashier, lowdowner buck nigger in dis community? Whar does the chicken feathers come from what I seen in his back yard dis mawnin'? Kin Brudder Wadkins rise and explain?"

Brother Wadkins sat in his pew with his eyes rolling and breathing hard, but was taken by surprise and did not respond.

"And dar is Elder Hoskins, on de right. Everybody knows he's er lying, shiftless, beer-drinking bum. His wife supports him takin' in washin'. What good is de blood of de Lamb done for him? Wonder ef he thinks dat he kin keep a lofin' 'round in de kitchen ob de New Jerusalem?"

Elder Hoskins, goaded by these charges, rose in his seat, and said:

"Dat reminds me ob one thing. I doesn't remember dat I hab ebber worked on de county road fur thirty days down in Bastrop County fur stealin' a bale of cotton."

"Who did? Who did?" said the parson, putting on his specs and glaring at the elder. "Who stole dat cotton? You shet yo' mouf, niggah, fo' I come down dah and bust you wide open. Den dar sets Miss Jinny Simpson. Look at dem fine clo'es she got on. Look at dem yallar shoes, and dem ostrick feathers, and dat silk waist and de white glubs. Whar she git de money to buy dem clo'es? She don't work none. De Lawd am got his eye on dat triflin' hussy, and He's gwine ter fling her in de burnin' brimstone and de squenchable pit."

Miss Simpson arose, her ostrich plumes trembling with indignation.

"You mis'able lyin' ol' niggah," she said. "You don' pay fur none ob my clo'es. S'pose you tells dis 'sembled congregation who was it handed dat big bouquet and dat jib ob cider ober de fence to Liza Jackson yisterday mawnin' when her old man gone to work?"

"Dat's a lie, you sneakin', low-down spyin' daughter ob de debble. I wuz in my house ras'lin in pra'er fur de wicked sisters and brudders ob dis church. I come down dah an' smack you in de mouf ef you don't shet up. You is all boun' for de fire ob destruction. You am all nothin' but vile sweepins ob de yearth. I see Bill Rodgers ober dar, who am known to hab loaded dice fur playin' craps, and he nebber pays a cent fur what his family eats. De Lawd am shore gwine ter smote him in de neck. De judgment ob de Spirit am gwine ter rise up an' call him down."

Bill Rodgers stood up and put his thumbs in the armholes of his vest. "I could name, sah," he said, "a certain party who wuz run off ob Colonel Yancy's fahm fo' playin' sebben up wid marked cya'ds, ef I choosed to."

"Dat's anudder lie," said the preacher, closing his Bible and turning up his cuffs. "Look out, Bill Rodgers, I'm comin' down dar to you."

The preacher got out of his pulpit and made for Bill, but Miss Simpson got her hands in his wool first, and Sam Wadkins and Elder Hoskins came quickly to her assistance. Then the rest of the brothers and sisters joined in, and the flying hymn books and the sound of ripping clothes testified to the fact that Sam Jones's style of preaching did not go in that particular church.

Superlatives

> *"I think the song that is sweetest*
> *Is the one that is never sung;*
> *That lies in the heart of the singer,*
> *Too grand for mortal tongue."*
>
> Some poet or other.

The hen egg that is largest
Was the one she never laid;
And the biggest bet in all the world
Was the one we never made.

And the biggest fight that Dallas had
Was the one that did not go;
And the finest poet in the world was the one
That didn't write "Beautiful Snow."

The finest country in all the world
Has never yet been explored,
And the finest artesian well in town
Has not at this time been bored.

By Easy Stages

"You're at the wrong place," said Cerberus. "This is the gate that leads to the infernal regions, while it is a passport to Heaven that you have handed me."

"I know it," said the departed shade wearily, "but it allows a stopover here; you see, I'm from Galveston and I have got to make the change gradually."

Even Worse

Two Houston men were going home one rainy night last week, and as they stumbled and plowed through the mud across one of the principal streets, one of them said:

"This is hell, isn't it?"

"Worse," said the other. "Even hell is paved with good intentions."

The Shock

A man with a very pale face, wearing a woolen comforter and holding a slender stick in his hand, staggered into a Houston drug store yesterday and leaned against the counter, holding the other hand tightly against his breast.

The clerk got a graduating glass, and poured an ounce of spiritus frumenti into it quickly, and handed it to him. The man drank it at a gulp.

"Feel better?" asked the clerk.

"A little. Don't know when I had such a shock. I can hardly stand. Just a little more, now—"

The clerk gave him another ounce of whisky.

"My pulse has started again, I believe," said the man. "It was terrible, though!"

"Fell off a wagon?" asked the clerk.

"No, not exactly."

"Slip on a banana peel?"

"I think not. I'm getting faint again, if you—"

The obliging clerk administered a third dose of the stimulant.

"Street car run over you?" he asked.

"No," said the pale man. "I'll tell you how it was. See that red-faced man out there swearing and dancing on the corner?"

"Yes."

"He did it. I don't believe I can stand up much longer. I—thanks."

The man tossed off the fourth reviver and began to look better.

"Shall I call a doctor?" asked the clerk.

"No, I guess not. Your kindness has revived me. I'll tell you about it. I have one of those toy spiders attached to a string at the end of this stick, and I saw that red-faced man sitting on a doorstep with his back to me, and I let the spider down over his head in front of his nose. I didn't know who he was, then.

"He fell over backwards and cut his ear on the foot-scraper and broke a set of sixty-dollar false teeth. That man is my landlord and I owe him $37 back rent, and he holds a ten-dollar mortgage on my cow, and has already threatened to break my back. I slipped in here and he hasn't seen me yet. The shock to my feelings when I saw who it was, was something awful. If you have a little more of that spirits now, I—"

The Cynic

Junior Partner: Here's an honest firm!

Sharp and Simpson send us a check for $50 in addition to their monthly account, to cover difference in price of a higher grade of goods shipped them last time by mistake.

Senior Partner: Do they give us another order?

Junior Partner: Yes! The longest they have ever made.

Senior Partner: Ship 'em COD.

"Well! how are they coming?"

"I'm getting a move on me," said the checkerboard.

"And I'm getting a head in the world," said the piece of sensation news.

"I'm dead in it," said the spoiled bivalve at the clambake.

"I think I shall get along well," said the artesian water company.

"And my work is all being cut out for me," said the grape seed.

Speaking of Big Winds

The man with the bronzed face and distinguished air was a great traveler, and had just returned from a tour around the world. He sat around the stove at the Lamlor, and four or five drummers and men about town listened with much interest to his tales.

He was speaking of the fierce wind storms that occur in South America, when the long grass of the pampas is interlaced and blown so flat by the hurricanes that it is cut into strips and sold for the finest straw matting.

He spoke also of the great intelligence of the wild cattle which, he said, although blown about by the furious hurricanes and compelled to drift for days before the drenching floods of the rainy season, never lost their direction by day or night.

"How do they guide themselves?" asked the Topeka flour drummer.

"Oh, by their udders, of course," said the traveler.

"I don't see anything to laugh about," said the Kansas man, "but speaking of big winds we have something of the kind in our state. You've all heard of the Kansas cyclones, but very few of you know what they are. We have plenty of them and some are pretty hard ones, too, but most of the stories you read about them are exaggerated. Still a good, full-grown cyclone can carry things pretty high sometimes. About the only thing they spend their fury upon in vain is a real estate agent. I know a fellow, named Bob Long, who was a real estate hustler from away back. Bob had bought up a lot of prairie land cheap, and was trying to sell it in small tracts for farms and truck patches. One day he took a man in his buggy out to this land and was showing it to him. 'Just look at it,' he said. 'It is the finest, richest piece of ground in Kansas. Now it's worth more, but to start things off, and get improvements to going, I'll sell you 160 acres of this land at $40 per—!'

"Before Bob could say 'acre,' a cyclone came along, and the edge of it took Bob up straight into the air. He went up till he was nothing but a black speck and the man stood there and watched him till he was out of sight.

"The man liked the land, so he bought it from Bob's heirs, and pretty soon a railroad cut across it, and a fine flourishing town sprang up on the spot.

"Well, this man was standing on the sidewalk one day thinking of how lucky he had been, and about Bob's unfortunate fate, when he happened to look up and saw something falling. It grew larger and larger, and finally it turned out to be a man.

"He came tumbling down, struck the sidewalk with a sound you could have heard four blocks away, bounded up at least ten feet, came down on his feet and shouted 'Front foot!'

"It was Bob Long. His beard was a little grayer and longer, but he was all business still. He had noticed the changes that had taken place while he was coming down, and when he finished the sentence that he began when the cyclone took him up, he altered his language accordingly. Bob was a hustler. Sometime after that he—"

"Never mind," said the traveler. "Let's go in and take something on this one first. I claim the usual time before the next round."

Unknown Title

An old woman who lived in Fla.
Had some neighbors who all the time ba
Tea, sugar, and soap
Till she said: "I do hope
I'll never see folks that are ha."

An Original Idea

There is a lady in Houston who is always having original ideas.

Now, this is a very reprehensible thing in a woman and should be frowned down. A woman should find out what her husband thinks about everything and regulate her thoughts to conform with his. Of course, it would not be so bad if she would keep her independent ideas to herself, but who ever knew a woman to do that?

This lady in particular had a way of applying her original ideas to practical use, and her family, and even neighbors, were kept constantly on the lookout for something startling at her hands.

One day she read in the columns of an Austin newspaper an article that caused her at once to conceive an original idea. The article called attention to the well-known fact that if men's homes supplied their wants and desires they would have no propensity to wander abroad, seeking distraction in gilded saloons. This struck the lady as a forcible truth, and she boldly plagiarized the idea and resolved to put it into immediate execution as an original invention.

That night when her husband came home he noticed a curtain stretched across one end of the sitting room, but he had so long been used to innovations of all sorts that he was rather afraid to investigate.

It might be stated apropos to the story that the lady's husband was addicted to the use of beer.

He not only liked beer, but he fondly loved beer. Beer never felt the slightest jealousy when this gentleman was out of its sight.

After supper the lady said: "Now, Robert, I have a little surprise for you. There is no need of your going downtown tonight, as you generally do, because I have arranged our home so that it will supply all the pleasures that you go out to seek."

With that she drew the curtain and Robert saw that one end of the sitting room had been fitted up as a bar—or rather his wife's idea of a bar.

A couple of strips of the carpet had been taken up and sawdust strewn on the floor. The kitchen table extended across the end of the room, and back of this on a shelf were arranged a formidable display of bottles, of all shapes and sizes, while the mirror of the best dresser had been taken off and placed artistically in the center.

On a trestle stood a fresh keg of beer and his wife, who had put on a coquettish-looking cap and apron, tripped lightly behind the bar, and waving a beer mug coyly at him said:

"It's an idea I had, Robert. I thought it would be much nicer to have you spend your money at home, and at the same time have all the amusement and pleasure that you do downtown. What will you have, sir?" she continued, with fine, commercial politeness.

Robert leaned against the bar and pawed the floor fruitlessly three or four times, trying to find the foot rest. He was a little stunned, as he always was at his wife's original ideas. Then he braced himself and tried to conjure up a ghastly imitation of a smile.

"I'll take a beer, please," he said.

His wife drew the beer, laid the nickel on the shelf and leaned on the bar, chatting familiarly on the topics of the day after the manner of bartenders.

"You must buy plenty, now," she said archly, "for you are the only customer I have tonight."

Robert felt a strong oppression of spirits, which he tried to hide. Besides the beer, which was first rate, there was little to remind him of the saloons where he had heretofore spent his money.

The lights, the glittering array of crystal, the rattle of dice, the funny stories of Brown, Jones, and Robinson, the motion and color that he found in the other places were wanting.

Robert stood still for quite a while and then an original idea struck him.

He pulled a handful of change from his pocket and began to call for glass after glass of beer. The lady behind the bar was beaming with pleasure at the success of her experiment. Ordinarily she had made quite a row, if her husband came home smelling of beer—but now, when the profits were falling into her own hands, she made no complaint.

It is not known how many glasses she sold her husband but there was quite a little pile of nickels and dimes on the shelf, and two or three quarters.

Robert was leaning rather heavily against the bar, now and then raising his foot and making a dab for the rod that was not there, but he was saying very little. His wife ought to have known better, but the profits rendered her indiscreet.

Presently Robert remarked in a very loud tone:

"Gozzamighty, se' 'm up all roun' barkeep'n puzzom on slate 'm busted."

His wife looked at him in surprise.

"Indeed, I will not, Robert," she said. "You must pay me for everything you have. I thought you understood that."

Robert looked in the mirror as straight as he could, counted his reflections, and then yelled loud enough to be heard a block away:

"Gosh dang it, gi' us six glasses beer and put 'em on ice, Susie, old girl, or I'll clean out your joint, 'n bus' up business. Whoopee!"

"Robert!" said his wife, in a tone implying a growing suspicion, "you've been drinking!"

"Zas d——d lie!" said Robert, as he threw a beer glass through the mirror. "Been down t' office helpin' friend pos' up books 'n missed last car. Say, now, Susie, old girl, you owe me two beers from las' time. Give 'em to me or I'll kick down bar."

Robert's wife was named Henrietta. When he made this remark she came around to the front and struck him over the eye with a lemon squeezer. Robert then kicked over the table, broke about half the bottles, spilled the beer, and used language not suited for the mailable edition.

Ten minutes later his wife had him tied with the clothes line, and during the intervals between pounding him on the head with a potato masher she was trying to think how to get rid of her last great original idea.

Calculations

A gentleman with long hair and an expression indicating heavenly resignation stepped off the twelve-thirty train at the Grand Central Depot yesterday. He had a little bunch of temperance tracts in his hand, and he struck a strong scent and followed it up to a red-nosed individual who was leaning on a trunk near the baggage room.

"My friend," said the long-haired man, "do you know that if you had placed the price of three drinks out at compound interest at the time of the building of Solomon's temple, you would now have $47,998,645.22?"

"I do," said the red-nosed man. "I am something of a calculator myself. I also figured out when the doctor insisted on painting my nose with iodine to cure that boil, that the first lanternjawed, bone-spavined, rubbernecked son-of-a-gun from the amen corner of Meddlesome County that made any remarks about it would have to jump seventeen feet in nine seconds or get kicked thirteen times below the belt. You have just four seconds left."

The long-haired man made a brilliant retreat within his allotted time, and bore down with his temperance tracts upon a suspicious-looking Houston man who was carrying home a bottle of mineral water wrapped in a newspaper to his mother-in-law.

A Valedictory

> *The "Some Postscripts" man on the* Post *has about reached the end of his vein. These spurts of brilliancy many are capable of, but the sustained light that burns for years to gladden and instruct is a rare quality, and the possessor should be appreciated by the people, for he is the true Messiah—the eldest son of the great intellectual lord of the universe.*
>
> Brenham Press

Brother, you should not have given us away. We just had to salt that vein before we could get it in the market, and when the "salt" gave out, and the end of the vein was reached, we hoped you wouldn't notice the fact. If you hadn't mentioned it we might have gone on for years gladdening and instructing and drawing princely salary, but now our little spurt of our brilliancy will have to put on its pajamas and retire between the cold sheets of oblivion. We do not blame you at all for calling the public's attention to the played-out lode, for it is a terrible responsibility to guide the footsteps of innocent purchasers who may be taken in by glittering, quartz and seductive pyrites of iron. To have one whom we regarded as a friend jerk us backward by the left leg when we had made such a successful sneak, and were about to scramble over the back fence of the temple of fame makes us sad, but we do not repine for:

> "'Twere better to have spurted and lost
> Than never to have spurted at all."

We really intended our light to burn for years, and to have the wick snuffed so quickly, although done in sorrowing kindness, causes us to sputter and smoke a little as we go out.

When the true Messiah comes along and shies his valise over to the night clerk, and turns back his cuffs ready to fill the long-felt want; if he should ever hear the whoops of those unappreciative critics who would crucify him, these few lines may teach him to fly to Brenham where his papa, the great intellectual lord of the universe, will protect him.

Solemn Thoughts

The golden crescent of the new moon hung above the market house, and the night was cool, springlike, and perfect.

Five or six men were sitting in front of the Hutchins House, and they had gradually shifted their chairs until they were almost in a group.

They were men from different parts of the country, some of them from cities thousands of miles away. They had been rattled in the dice box of chance and thrown in a temporary cluster into the hospitable gates of the Magnolia city.

They smoked and talked, and that feeling of comradeship which seizes men who meet in the world far from their own homes, was strong upon them.

They told all their funny stories and compared experiences, and then a little silence fell upon them, and while the hanging strata of blue smoke grew thicker, their thoughts began to wander back—as the cows stray homeward at eventide—to other scenes and faces.

> "'And o'er them many a flaming range of vapor buoyed
> the crescent bark:
> And rapt through many a rosy change
> The twilight melted into dark,'"

quoted the New York drummer. "Heigho! I wish I was at home tonight."

"Same here," said the little man from St. Louis. "I can just see the kids now tumbling round on the floor and cutting up larks before Laura puts them to bed. There's one blessing, though, I'll be home on Thanksgiving."

"I had a letter from home today," said the white-bearded Philadelphian, "and it made me homesick. I would give a foot of that slushy pavement on Spruce Street for all these balmy airs and mockingbird solos in the South. I'm going to strike a bee line for the Quaker City in time for that fat turkey, I don't care what my house says."

"Yust hear dot band playing," said the fat gentleman. "I can almost dink I vos back in Cincinnati 'neber die Rhein' mit dot schplendid little beautiful girl from de hat factory. I dink it is dese lovely nights vot makes us of home, sweet home, gedinken."

"Now you're shoutin'," said the Chicago hardware drummer. "I wish I was in French Pete's restaurant on State Street with a big bottle of beer and some chitterlings and lemon pie. I'm feelin' kinder sentimental myself tonight."

"The worst part of it is," said the man with the gold nose glasses and green necktie, "that our dear ones are separated from us by many long and dreary miles, and we little know what obstacles in the shape of storm and flood and wreck lie in our way. If we could but annihilate time and space for a brief interval there are many of us who would clasp the forms of those we love to our hearts tonight. I, too, am a husband and father."

"That breeze," said the man from New York, "feels exactly like the ones that used to blow over the old farm in Montgomery County, and that 'orchard and meadow, and deep tangled wildwood,' etc., keep bobbing up in my memory tonight."

"How many of us," said the man with gold glasses, "realize the many pitfalls that Fate digs in our path? What a slight thing may sever the cord that binds us to life! There today, tomorrow gone forever from the world!"

"Too true," said the Philadelphia man, wiping his spectacles.

"And leave those we love behind," continued the other. "The affections of a lifetime, the love of the strongest hearts, ended in the twinkling of an eye. One loses the clasp of hands that would detain and drifts away into the sad, unknowable, other existence, leaving aching hearts to mourn forever. Life seems all a tragedy."

"Banged if you ain't rung the bell first shot," said the Chicago drummer. "Our affections get busted up something worse'n killing hogs."

The others frowned upon the Chicago drummer, for the man with gold glasses was about to speak again.

"We say," he went on, "that love will live forever, and yet when we are gone others step into our places and the wounds our loss had made are healed. And yet there is an added pang to death that those of us that are wise can avoid, the sting of death and the victory of the grave can be lessened. When we know that our hours are numbered, and when we lie with ebbing breath and there comes

> 'Unto dying ears the earliest pipe
> Of half awakened birds;
> And unto dying eyes
> The casement slowly grows a glimmering square,'

there is sweet relief in knowing that those we leave behind us are shielded from want.

"Gentlemen, we are all far from home and you know the risks of travel. I am representing one of the best accident insurance companies on earth, and I want to write every one of you. I offer you the finest death, partial disablement, loss of finger or toe, nervous shock, sick benefit policy known to—"

But the man with gold spectacles was talking to five empty chairs, and the moon slipped down below the roof of the market house with a sardonic smile.

Explaining It

A member of the Texas Legislature from one of the eastern counties was at the chrysanthemum show at Turner Hall last Thursday night, and was making himself agreeable to one of the lady managers.

"You were in the House at the last session, I believe?" she inquired.

"Well, madam," he said, "I was in the House, but the Senate had me for about forty-five dollars when we adjourned."

Her Failing

They were two Houston girls, and they were taking a spin on their wheels. They met a fluffy girl who didn't "bike," out driving with a young man in a buggy.

Of course they must say something about her—as this is a true story and they were real, live girls—so one of them said:

"I never did like that girl."

"Why?"

"Oh, she's too effeminate."

A Disagreement

"Dat Mr. Bergman, vot run de obera house, not dread me right," said a Houston citizen. "Ven I go dere und vant ein dicket to see dot 'Schpider und dot Vly' gompany de oder night, I asg him dot he let me in mit half brice, for I was teaf py von ear, and can not but one half of dot performance hear; und he dell me I should bay double brice, as it vould dake me dwice as long to hear de berformance as anypody else."

An E for a Knee

When Pilgrim fathers landed safe
On Plymouth Rock at last,
They bowed their heads and bent a knee,
And kept a holy fast.

But now to celebrate the day
We dine—to say the least—
We add an "e" into their plan
And change their fast to feast.

The Unconquerable

A man may avoid the Nin-com-poop
By flying fast and far.
And even subdue the Scalawag
By stratagems of war.

And he even may dodge the Fly-up-the-Creek
If he's lucky and does not fear;
And sometimes conquer the powerful chump.
Though the victory cost him dear.

And a brave man may do up the Galoot,
Though it be a terrible fight,
But no man yet has escaped from the clutch
Of the terrible Blatherskite.

An Expensive Veracity

A Houston man who attended a great many of Sam Jones's sermons was particularly impressed with his denunciation of prevaricators, and of lies of all kinds, white, variegated, and black.

So strongly was he affected and in such fertile ground did the seed sown by the great evangelist fall, that the Houston man, who had been accustomed occasionally to evade the truth, determined one morning he would turn over a new leaf and tell the truth in all things, big and little. So he commenced the day by scorning to speak even a word that did not follow the exact truth for a model.

At breakfast, his wife said:

"How are the biscuit, Henry?"

"Rather heavy," he answered, "and about half done."

His wife flounced out of the dining room and he ate breakfast with the children. Ordinarily Henry would have said, "They are very fine, my dear," and all would have been well.

As he went out the gate, his rich old aunt, with whom he had always been a favorite, drove up. She was curled, and stayed, and powdered to look as young as possible.

"Oh, Henry," she simpered. "How are Ella and the children? I would come in but I'm looking such a fright today I'm not fit to be seen."

"Yes," said Henry, "you do. It's a good thing your horse has a blind bridle on, for if he got a sight of you he'd run away and break your neck."

His aunt glared furiously at him and drove away without saying a word.

Henry figured it up afterward and found that every word he said to her cost him $8,000.

Grounds for Uneasiness

When Sousa's Band was in Houston a week or so ago, Professor Sousa was invited to dine with a prominent citizen who had met him while on a visit to the North.

This gentleman, while a man of high standing and reputation, has made quite a fortune by the closest kind of dealing. His economies in the smallest matters are a fruitful subject of discussion in his neighborhood, and one or two of his acquaintances have gone so far as to call him stingy.

After dinner Professor Sousa was asked to play upon the piano, of which instrument he is a master, and he did so, performing some lovely Beethoven sonatas, and compositions by the best masters.

While playing a beautiful adagio movement in a minor key, the Professor caught sight of his host casting uneasy glances out of the window and appearing very restless and worried. Presently the Houston gentleman came over to the piano and touched Professor Sousa on the shoulder.

"Say," he said, "please play something livelier. Give us a jig or a quickstep—something fast and jolly."

"Ah," said the Professor, "this sad music affects your spirits then?"

"No," said the host, "I've got a man in the back yard sawing wood by the day, and he's been keeping time to your music for the last half hour."

It Covers Errors

Poetic fame can be won this way:
If you happen to have not a thing to say,
And you happen to be close-pressed for time,
And you can't for your life get a word to rhyme,
And your knowledge of English is somewhat small,
And you have no poetic turn at all,
And can't write a hand anybody can read.
You are in a first-rate way to succeed;
For who in the world can mix things worse
Than a popular writer of dialect verse?

Recognition

The new woman came in with a firm and confident tread. She hung her hat on a nail, stood her cane in the corner, and kissed her husband gayly as he was mixing the biscuit for supper.

"Any luck today, dearie?" asked the man as his careworn face took on an anxious expression.

"The best of luck," she said with a joyous smile. "The day has come when the world recognizes woman as man's equal in everything. She is no longer content to occupy a lower plane than his, and is his competitor in all the fields of action. I obtained a position today at fifty dollars per week for the entire season."

"What is the position?"

"Female impersonator at the new theater."

His Doubt

They lived in a neat little cottage on Prairie Avenue, and had been married about a year. She was young and sentimental and he was a clerk at fifty dollars per month. She sat rocking the cradle and looking at a bunch of something pink and white that was lying asleep, and he was reading the paper.

"Charlie," she said, presently, "you must begin to realize that you must economize and lay aside something each month for the future. You must realize that the new addition to our home that will bring us joy arid pleasure and make sweet music around our fireside must be provided for. You must be ready to meet the obligations that will be imposed upon you, and remember that another than ourselves must be considered, and that as our hands strike the chords so shall either harmony or discord be made, and as the notes mount higher and higher, we shall be held to account for our trust here below. Do you realize the responsibility?"

Charlie said "Yes," and then went out in the woodshed and muttered to himself: "I wonder whether she was talking about the kid, or means to buy a piano on the installment plan."

A Cheering Thought

A weary-looking man with dejected auburn whiskers, walked into the police station yesterday afternoon and said to the officer in charge:

"I want to give myself up. I expect you had better handcuff me and put me into a real dark cell where there are plenty of spiders and mice. I'm one of the worst men you ever saw, and I waive trial. Please tell the jailer to give me moldy bread to eat, and hydrant water with plenty of sulphur in it."

"What have you done?" asked the officer.

"I'm a miserable, low-down, lying, good-for-nothing, slandering, drunken, villainous, sacrilegious galoot, and I'm not fit to die. You might ask the jailer, also, to bring little boys in to look at me through the bars, while I gnash my teeth and curse in demoniac rage."

"We can't put you in jail unless you have committed some offense. Can't you bring some more specific charge against yourself?"

"No, I just want to give myself up on general principles. You see, I went to hear Sam Jones last night, and he saw me in the crowd and diagnosed my case to a *T*. Up to that time I thought I was a four-horse team with a yellow dog under the wagon, but Sam took the negative side and won. I'm a danged old sore-eyed hound dog; I wouldn't mind if you kicked me a few times before you locked me up, and sent my wife word that the old villain that has been abusin' her for twenty years has met his deserts."

"Aw, come now," said the officer, "I don't believe you are as bad as you think you are. You don't know that Sam Jones was talking about you at all. It might have been somebody else he was hitting. Brace up and don't let it worry you."

"Lemme see," said the weary-looking man reflectively. "Come to think of it there was one of my neighbors sitting right behind me who is the meanest man in Houston. He is a mangy pup, and no mistake. He beats his wife and has refused to loan me three dollars five different times. What Sam said just fits his case exactly. If I thought now—"

"That's the way to look at it," said the officer. "The chances are Sam wasn't thinking about you at all."

"Durned if I believe he was, now I remember about that neighbor of mine," said the penitent, beginning to brighten up. "You don't know what a weight you've taken off my mind. I was just feeling like I was one of the worst sinners in the world. I'll bet any man ten dollars he was talking right straight at that miserable, contemptible scalawag that sat right behind me. Say, come on and let's go out and take somethin', will you?"

The officer declined and the weary-looking man ran his finger down his neck and pulled his collar up into sight and said:

"I'll never forget your kindness, sir, in helping me out of this worry. It has made me feel bad all day. I am going out to the racetrack now, and take the field against the favorite for a few plunks. Good day, I shall always remember your kindness."

What It Was

There was something the matter with the electric lights Tuesday night, and Houston was as dark as Egypt when Moses blew the gas out. They were on Rusk Avenue, out on the lawn, taking advantage of the situation, and were holding as close a session as possible.

Presently she said:

"George, I know you love me, and I am sure that nothing in the world can change my affection for you, yet I feel that something has come between us, and although I have hesitated long to tell you, it is paining me very much."

"What is it, my darling?" asked George, in an agony of suspense. "Speak, my own, and tell me what it is that has come between you and me?"

"I think, George" she softly sighed, "it is your watch."

And George loosened his hold for a moment and shifted his Waterbury.

Vanity

A poet sang a song so wondrous sweet,
That toiling thousands paused and listened long;
So lofty, strong, and noble were his themes,
It seemed that strength supernal swayed his song.

He, god-like, chided poor, weak, weeping man,
And bade him dry his foolish, shameful tears.
Taught that each soul on its proud self should lean,
And from that rampart scorn all earth-born fears.

The poet groveled on a fresh-heaped mound
Raised o'er the grave of one he fondly loved,
And cursed the world, and drenched the sod with tears,
And all the flimsy mockery of his precepts proved.

Identified

A stranger walked into a Houston bank the other day and presented a draft to the cashier for payment.

"You will have to be identified," said the cashier, "by someone who knows your name to be Henry B. Saunders."

"But I don't know anybody in Houston," said the stranger. "Here's a lot of letters addressed to me, and a telegram from my firm, and a lot of business cards. Won't they be identification enough?"

"I am sorry," said the cashier, "but while I have no doubt that you are the party, our rule is to require better identification."

The man unbuttoned his vest and showed the initial, H. B. S., on his shirt. "Does that go?" he asked. The cashier shook his head. "You might have Henry B. Saunders' letters, and his papers, and also his shirt on, without being the right man. We are forced to be very careful."

The stranger tore open his shirt front, and exhibited a large mustard plaster, covering his entire chest. "There," he shouted, "if I wasn't Henry B. Saunders, do you suppose I would go around wearing one of his mustard plasters stuck all over me? Do you think I would carry my impersonation of anybody far enough to blister myself to look like him? Gimme tens and fives, now, I haven't got time to fool any more."

The cashier hesitated and then shoved out the money. After the stranger had gone, the official rubbed his chin gently and said softly to himself: "That plaster might be somebody else's after all, but no doubt it's all right."

The Apple

A youth held in his hand a round, red, luscious apple.

"Eat," said the Spirit, "it is the apple of life."

"I will have none of it," said the Youth, and threw it far from him. "I will have success. I will have fame, fortune, power and knowledge."

"Come, then," said the Spirit.

They went together up steep and rocky paths. The sun scorched, the rain fell upon them, the mountain mists clung about them, and the snow fell in beautiful and treacherous softness, obscuring the way as they climbed. Time swiftly passed and the golden locks of the Youth took on the whiteness of the snow. His form grew bent with the toil of climbing; his hand grew weak and his voice quivering and high.

The Spirit had not changed and upon his face was the inscrutable smile of wisdom.

They stood at last upon the topmost peak. The old man that was the Youth said to the Spirit: "Give me the apple of Success. I have come upon the heights where it grows and it is mine. Be quick, for there is a strange dimness in my sight."

The Spirit gave him an apple round and red and fair to behold.

The man bit into it and found rottenness and bitter dust.

"What is this?" he asked.

"It was the apple of Life," said the Spirit. "It is now the apple of Success."

How It Started

"You had better move your chair a little further back," said the old resident. "I saw one of the Judkinses go into the newspaper office just now with his gun, and there may be some shooting."

The reporter, who was in the town gathering information for the big edition, got his chair quickly behind a pillar of the hotel piazza, and asked what the trouble was about.

"It's an old feud of several years' standing," said the old resident, "between the editor and the Judkins family. About every two months they get to shooting at one another. Everybody in town knows about it. This is the way it started. The Judkinses live in another town, and one time a good-looking young lady of the family came here on a visit to a Mrs. Brown. Mrs. Brown gave her a big party—a regular high-toned affair, to get the young men acquainted with her. One young fellow fell in love with her, and sent a little poem to our paper, the *Observer.* This is the way it read:

To Miss Judkins
(Visiting Mrs. T. Montcalm Brown.)

"We love to see her wear
A gown of simple white.
Nothing but a rose in her hair
At Mrs. Brown's that night,
The fairest of them all
She stood, with blushes red,
While bright the gaslight shone
Upon her lovely head.

"That poem, now, was what started the feud."

"I don't see anything wrong with the poem," said the reporter. "It seems a little crude, but contains nothing to give offense."

"Well," said the old resident, "the poem was all right as it was written. The trouble originated in the newspaper office. The morning after it was sent in the society editress got hold of it first. She is an old maid and she didn't think the second line quite proper, so she ran her pencil through it. Then the advertising manager prowled around through the editor's mail as usual, and read the poem. Old Brown owed the office $17 back subscription, and the advertising manager struck out the fourth line. He said old Brown shouldn't get any free advertising in that office.

"Then the editor's wife happened to come in to see if there was any square, perfumed envelopes among his mail, and she read it. She was at the Brown's party herself, and when she read the line that proclaimed Miss Judkins 'The fairest of them all' she turned up her nose and scratched that out.

"Then the editor himself got hold of it. He is heavily interested in our new electric light plant, and his blue pencil jumped on the line 'While bright the gaslight shone' in a hurry. Later on one of the printers came in and grabbed a lot of copy, and this poem was among it. You know what printers will do if you give them a chance, so here is the way the poem came out in the paper:

> To Miss Judkins
> (Visiting Mrs. T. Montcalm Brown.)
>
> "We loved to see her wear
> Nothing but a rose in her hair.
> She stood with blushes red
> Upon her lovely head.

"And you see," continued the old resident, "the Judkinses got mad."

Red Conlin's Eloquence

They were speaking of the power of great orators, and each one had something to say of his especial favorite.

The drummer was for backing Bourke Cockran for oratory against the world, the young lawyer thought the suave Ingersoll the most persuasive pleader, and the insurance agent advanced the claims of the magnetic W. C. P. Breckenridge.

"They all talk some," said the old cattle man, who was puffing his pipe and listening, "but they couldn't hold a candle to Red Conlin, that run cattle below Santone in '80. Ever know Red?"

Nobody had had the honor.

"Red Conlin was a natural orator; he wasn't overcrowded with book learnin', but his words come free and easy, like whisky out of a new faucet from a full barrel. He was always in a good humor and smilin' clear across his face, and if he asked for a hot biscuit he did it like he was pleadin' for his life. He was one man who had the gift of gab, and it never failed him.

"I remember once, in Atascosa County, the hoss thieves worried us right smart. There was a gang of 'em, and they got runnin' off a caballaro every week or so. Some of us got together and raised a p'int of order and concluded to sustain it. The head of the gang was a fellow named Mullens, and a tough cuss he was. Fight, too, and warn't particular when. Twenty of us saddled up and went into camp, loaded down with six-shooters and Winchesters. That Mullens had the nerve to try to cut off our saddle horses the first night, but we heard him, got mounted, and went hot on his trail. There was five or six others with Mullens.

"It was dark as thunder, and pretty soon we run one of them down. His horse was lame, and we knew it was Mullens by his big white hat and black beard. We didn't hardly give him time to speak, we was so mad, but in two minutes there was a rope 'round his neck and Mullens was swung up at last. We waited about ten minutes till he was still, and then some fellow strikes a match out of curiosity and screeches out:

"'Gosh a'mighty, boys, we've strung up the wrong man!"

"And we had.

"We reopened the fellow's case and give him a new trial, and acquitted him, but it was too late to do him any good. He was as dead as Davy Crockett.

"It was Sandy McNeagh, one of the quietest, straightest, and best-respected men in the county, and what was worse, hadn't been married but about three months.

"'Whatever are we to do?' says I, and it sure was a case to think about.

"'We ought to be nigh Sandy's house now,' said one of the men, who was tryin' to peer around and kind of locate the scene of our brilliant coop detaw, as they say.

"Just then we seen a light from a door that opened in the dark, and the house wasn't two hundred yards away, and we saw what we knew must be Sandy's wife in the door a-lookin' for him.

"'Somebody's got to go and tell her,' said I. I was kind o' leadin' the boys. 'Who'll do it?' Nobody jumped at the proposition.

"'Red Conlin' says I, 'you're the man to tell her, and the only man here what could open his mouth to the poor girl. Go, like a man, and may the Lord teach you what to say, for d——d if I can.'

"That boy never hesitated. I saw him kind o' wet his hand, and smooth back his red curls in the dark, and I seen his teeth shinin' as he said:

"'I'll go, boys; wait for me.'

"He went and we saw the door open and let him in.

"'May the Lord help that poor widder,' we all said, 'and d——n us for bunglin', murderin' butchers what ain't no right to call ourselves men.'

"It was fifteen minutes, maybe, when Red came back.

"'How is it'?' we whispered, almost afraid to hear him speak.

"'It's fixed,' says Red, 'and the widdy and I asks ye to the weddin' nixt Chuesday night.'

"That fellow Red Conlin could talk."

Why He Hesitated

A man with a worn, haggard countenance that showed traces of deep sorrow and suffering rushed excitedly up the stairs into the editorial rooms of the Post.

The literary editor was alone in his corner and the man threw himself into a chair nearby and said:

"Excuse me, sir, for inflicting my troubles upon you, but I must unbosom myself to someone. I am the unhappiest of men. Two months ago, in a quiet little town in Eastern Texas, there was a family dwelling in the midst of peace and contentment. Hezekiah Skinner was the head of that family, and he almost idolized his wife, who appeared to completely return his affection. Alas, sir, she was deceiving him. Her protestations of love were but honeyed lies, intended to beguile and blind him. She had become infatuated with William Wagstaff, a neighbor, who had insidiously planned to capture her affections. She listened to Wagstaff's pleadings and fled with him, leaving her husband with a wrecked home and a broken heart. Can you not feel for me, sir?"

"I do, indeed," said the literary editor. "I can conceive the agony, the sorrow, the deep suffering that you must have felt."

"For two months," continued the man, "the home of Hezekiah Skinner has been desolate, and this woman and Wagstaff have been flying from his wrath."

"What do you intend to do?" asked the literary editor.

"I scarcely know. I do not care for the woman any longer, but I cannot escape the tortures my mind is undergoing day after day."

At this point a shrill woman's voice was heard in the outer office, making some inquiry of the office boy.

"Great heavens, her voice!" said the man, rising to his feet greatly agitated. "I must get out of here. Quick! Is there no way for me to escape? A window—a side door—anywhere before she finds me."

The literary editor rose with indignation in his face.

"For shame, sir," he said, "do not act so unworthy a part. Confront your faithless wife, Mr. Skinner, and denounce her for wrecking your life and home. Why do you hesitate to stand up for your honor and your rights?"

"You do not understand," said the man, his face white with fear and apprehension, as he climbed out the window upon a shed. "I am William Wagstaff."

Turkish Questions

Oh, Sultan, tell us quick, we pray
What was it Pasha Said?
And have they burned the vilayet?
So many tales we've read.

Who was it passed the Dardanelles?
And were they counterfeit?
And why was Kharput beaten so?
Was there much dust in it?

Oh, Ottoman, to do like you
Who Hassan eye to see
The woes your country has to hear—
Armenia heart must be!

And tell us, is the Bosphorus?
Or is it still for you?
Why is it that you every day
Mustafa head or two?

Somebody Lied

Two men went into a saloon on Main Street yesterday and braced up solemnly to the bar. One was an old man with gray whiskers, the other was a long, lanky youth, evidently his son. Both were dressed like farm hands and they appeared somewhat bewildered at the splendor of the saloon.

The bartender asked them what they would have.

The old man leaned across the bar and said hoarsely and mysteriously: "You see, mister, me an' Lem just sold a load of tomatters and green corn fer nineteen dollars en a half. The old woman at home figgered we'd git just sixteen dollars and a quarter fer the truck, so me and Lem is three twenty-five ahead. When folks makes a big strike they most al'ays gets drunk, and es me and Lem never was drunk, we says, we'll git drunk and see how it feels. The feelin's pretty bully, ain't it?"

"Some think so," said the bartender, "what'll you have?"

They both called for whisky and stood against the bar until they had taken some five or six drinks apiece.

"Feel good, Lem?" asked the old man.

"Not a dam bit," said the son.

"Don't feel like shoutin' and raisin' Cain?"

"No."

"Don't feel good at all?"

"No. Feel like the devil. Feel sick, en burnin' inside."

"Is yer head buzzin', Lem, and er achin'?"

"Yes, Dad, en is yer knees a kind er wobblin', en yer eyes a waterin'?"

"You bet, en is yer stummick er gripin' en does yer feel like yer had swallowed a wild cat en er litter of kittens?"

"Yes, Dad, and don't you wish we wuz to home, whar we could lie down in ther clover patch en kick?"

"Yes, sonny, this here is what comes of goin' back on yer ma. Does yer feel real bad?"

"Bad ez ther devil, Dad."

"Look a here, mister," said the old man to the bartender, "somebody has lied to us about the fun in gettin' drunk. We're a goin' home and never goin' to do it again. I'd ruther hev the blind staggers, the itch, en the cramp colic all to onct, then ter git drunk. Come on, sonny, en let's hunt the waggin."

Marvelous

There is one man we know who is about as clever a reasoner as this country has yet produced. He has a way of thinking out a problem that is sometimes little short of divination. One day last week his wife told him to make some purchases, and as with all his logical powers he is rather forgetful on ordinary subjects, she tied a string around his finger so he would not forget his errand. About nine o'clock that night while hurrying homeward, he suddenly felt the string on his finger and stopped short. Then for the life of him he could not remember for what purpose the string had been placed there.

"Let's see," he said. "The string was tied on my finger so I would not forget. Therefore it is a forget-me-not. Now forget-me-not is a flower. Ah, yes, that's it. I was to get a sack of flour."

The giant intellect had got in its work.

The Confession of a Murderer

He is dead and I killed him.

I gaze upon him, lying cold and still, with the crimson blood welling from his wound, and I laugh with joy. On my hand his life blood leaped and I hold it proudly aloft bearing it accusing stain and in my heart there is no pity, no remorse, no softness. Seeing him lie there crushed and pulseless is to me more than the pleasure of paradise. For months he escaped me. With all the intense hate I bore him at times, I felt admiration for his marvelous courage, his brazen effrontery, his absolute ignorance of fear. Why did I kill him? Because he had with a fixed purpose and a diabolical, persistent effrontery, conspired to rob me of that which is as dear to me as my life. Brave as I have said he was, he scarcely dared to cross my path openly, but with insidious cunning had ever sought to strike me a blow in the dark.

I did not fear him, but I knew his power, and I dared not give him his opportunity.

Many a sleepless night I have spent, planning some means to rid myself of his devilish machinations. He even attempted to torture me by seeking to harm her whom I love. He approached herewith the utmost care and cunning, wearing the guise of a friend, but striving to instill his poison into her innocent heart.

But, thank heaven, she was faithful and true and his honeyed songs and wiles had no effect. When she would tell me of his approaches, how I would grind my teeth and clench my hands in fury, and long for the time when I would wreak a just vengeance upon him. The time has come. I found him worn and helpless from cold and hunger, but there was no pity in my heart. I struck him down and reveled with heartfelt joy when I saw him sink down, bathed in blood, and die by my hands. I do not fear the consequences. When I tell my tale I will be upheld by all.

He is dead and I am satisfied.

I think he is the largest and fattest mosquito I ever saw.

"Get Off the Earth"

"Get off the earth," says I,
"With your muddy boots and your dirty face;
Such a bother I never see,
You're the biggest torment in the place;
Forever worryin' an' pesterin' me.

"Get off the earth," says I.
I didn't mean that, but I was so vexed
At the boy's disturbin' way;
I never knew what he would do next
In his noisy, mischief-makin' play.

"Get off the earth," says I.
And that very night the fever came;
And now I'm cryin' to heaven in vain
For just one more touch of them same
Lost little grimy hands again.

The Stranger's Appeal

He was tall and angular and had a keen gray eye and a solemn face. His dark coat was buttoned high and had something of a clerical cut. His pepper and salt trousers almost cleared the tops of his shoes, but his tall hat was undeniably respectable, and one would have said he was a country preacher out for a holiday. He was driving a light wagon, and he stopped and climbed out when he came up to where five or six men were sitting on the post-office porch in a little country town in Texas.

"My friends," he said, "you all look like intelligent men, and I feel it my duty to say a few words to you in regard to the terrible and deplorable state of things now existing in this section of the country. I refer to the horrible barbarities recently perpetrated in the midst of some of the most civilized of Texas towns, when human beings created in the image of their Maker were subjected to cruel torture and then inhumanly burned in the public streets. Something must be done to wipe the stigma from the fair name of your state. Do you not agree with me?"

"Are you from Galveston, stranger?" asked one of the men.

"No, sir. I am from Massachusetts, the cradle of liberty of the downtrodden negro, and the home of the champions of his cause. These burnings are causing us to weep tears of blood and I am here to see if I can not move your hearts to pity on his behalf."

"I guess you might as well drive on," said one of the group. "We are going to look out for ourselves and just so long as negroes keep on committing the crimes they have, just so long will we punish them."

"And you will not repent of the lives you have taken by the horrible agency of fire?"

"Nary repent."

"And you will continue to visit upon them the horrible suffering of being burned to death?"

"If the occasion demands it."

"Well, then, gentlemen, since you are so determined, I want to sell you a few gross of the cheapest matches you ever laid your eyes upon. Step out to the wagon and see them. Warranted not to go out in a strong wind, and to strike on anything, wood, bricks, glass, bloomers, boot soles and iron. How many boxes will you take, gentlemen?"

The Good Boy

(Mostly in Words of One Syllable)

James was a good boy.

He w'ould not tease his cat or his dog.

He went to school.

One day as he went home he saw a lady cross the street, and some rude boys tried to guy her.

James took the lady by the hand and led her to a safe place.

"Oh, fie!" he said to the boys. "For shame, to talk so to the nice lady. A good, kind boy will be mild and love to help the old."

At this the boys did rail and laugh.

"Oh, boys," said James, "do not be rude and speak so harsh. At home, I have a dear old grandma, and this kind lady may be one, too."

The lady took James by the ear and said: "You contemptible little rapscallion. I've a good mind to spank you until you can't navigate. Grandmother, indeed! I'm only twenty-nine my last birthday, and I don't feel a day over eighteen. Now, you clear out, or I'll slap you good."

The Colonel's Romance

They were sitting around a stove and the tobacco was passed around. They began to grow introspective.

The talk turned upon their old homes and the changes that the cycling years bring about. They had lived in Houston for many years, but only one was a native Texan.

The colonel hailed from Alabama, the judge was born in the swamps of Mississippi, the grocer first saw the light in a frozen town of Maine, and the major proudly claimed Tennessee as his birthplace.

"Have any of you fellows been back home since you left there?" asked the colonel.

The judge had been back twice in twenty years, the major once, the grocer never.

"It's a curious feeling," said the colonel, "to go back to the old home where you were raised, after an absence of fifteen years. It is like seeing ghosts to be among people whom you have not seen in so long a time. Now I went back to Crosstree, Alabama, just fifteen years after I left there. The impression made upon me was one that never will be obliterated.

"There was a girl in Crosstree once that I loved better than anything in the world. One day I slipped away from everybody and went down to the little grove where I used to walk with her. I walked along the paths we used to tread. The oaks along the side had scarcely changed; the little blue flowers on either hand might have been the same ones she used to twine in her hair when she came to meet me.

"Our favorite walk had been along a line of thick laurels beyond which ran a little stream. Everything was the same. There was no change there to oppress my heart. Above were the same great sycamores and poplars; there ran the same brook; my feet trod the same path they had so often walked with her. It seemed that if I waited she would surely come again, tripping so lightly through the gloaming with her starry eyes, and nut-brown curls, and she loved me, too. It seemed then that nothing could ever have parted us—no doubt, no misunderstanding, no falsehood. But who can tell?

"I went to the end of the path. There stood the old hollow tree in which we used to place notes to each other. What sweet words that old tree could tell if it had known! I had fancied that during the rubs and knocks I had received from the world my heart had grown calloused, but such was not the case.

"I looked down into the hollow of the tree, and saw something white. It was a folded piece of paper, yellow and stained with age. I opened it and read it with difficulty.

> "'Dearest Richard: You know I will marry you if you want me to. Come round early tonight and I will give you my answer in a better way. Your own Nellie.'

"Gentlemen, I stood there holding that little piece of paper in my hand like one in a dream. I had written her a note asking her to marry me and telling her to leave her answer in the old tree. She must have done so, and I never got it, and all those years had rolled away since."

The crowd was silent. The major wiped his eyes, and the judge sniffed a little. They were middle-aged men now, but they, too, had known love.

"And then," said the grocer, "you left right away for Texas and never saw her again?"

"No," said the colonel. "When I didn't come round that night she sent her father after me, and we were married two months later. She and the five kids are up at the house now. Pass the tobacco, please."

A Narrow Escape

A meek-looking man, with one eye and a timid, shuffling gait, entered a Houston saloon while no one was in except the bartender, and said:

"Excuse me, sir, but would you permit me to step behind the bar for just a moment? You can keep your eye on me. There is something there I wanted to look at."

The bartender was not busy, and humored him through curiosity.

The meek-looking man stepped around and toward the shelf back of the bar.

"Would you kindly remove that wine bottle and those glasses for a moment?"

The bartender did so, and disclosed a little plowed streak on the shelf and a small hole bored for quite a distance into the wall.

"Thanks, that's all," said the meek man, as he went around to the front again.

He leaned thoughtfully on the bar and said: "I shot that hole in there just nine years ago. I came in feeling pretty thirsty and had no money. The bartender refused me a drink and I commenced firing. That ball went through his ear and five bottles of champagne before it stopped. I then yelled quite loudly, and two men broke their arms trying to get out the door, and the bartender trembled so when he mixed a drink for me you would have thought he was putting up a milk shake for a girl who wanted to catch a street car."

"Yes?" said the bartender.

"Yes, sir, I am feeling a little out of sorts today, and it always makes me real cross and impatient when I get that way. A little gin and bitters always helps me. It was six times, I think, that I fired, the time I was telling you about. Straight whisky would do if the gin is out."

"If I had any fly paper," said the bartender, sweetly, "I would stick you on it and set you in the back window; but I am out, consequently, I shall have to adopt harsher measures. I shall tie a knot in this towel, and then count ten, and walk around the end of the bar. That will give you time to do your shooting, and I'll see that you let out that same old yell that you spoke of."

"Wait a moment," said the meek man. "Come to think of it, my doctor ordered me not to drink anything for six weeks. But you had a narrow escape all the same. I think I shall go down to the next drug store and fall in a fit on the sidewalk. That's good for some peppermint and aromatic spirits of ammonia, anyhow."

A Years Supply

He was one of the city's wealthiest men, but he made no ostentatious display of his wealth. A little, thin, poorly clad girl stood looking in the window of the restaurant at the good things to eat. The man approached and touched her on the shoulder.

"What is your name, little girl?" he asked.

"Susie Tompkins, sir," she answered, looking up at him with great, haunting, blue eyes.

There was something in her pleading, innocent voice that stirred a strange feeling in the millionaire's heart. Still it may have been indigestion.

"Have you a father?" he asked.

"Oh, no, sir, mother has only me to support."

"Is your mother very poor?"

"Oh, yes, sir."

"What is your mother's name?"

"Susan, sir. Just like mine."

"Tell me, child," said the wealthy man, clutching her arm in an agony of suspense. "Has your mother a wart on her nose, and does her breath smell of onions?"

"Yes, sir."

The millionaire covered his face with his hands for a moment, and then said in a trembling voice:

"Little one, your mother and I once knew each other. You have her voice, her hair, and her eyes. If it had not been for a misunderstanding—perhaps—but that is all past now."

The man unbuttoned his overcoat and took from his vest pocket a package.

"Take this," he said. "I have more than I want. It will last you and your mother a year."

The little girl took the package and ran home in glee.

"Oh, see, mama!" she cried. "A gentleman gave me this. He said it would last us a whole year."

The pale woman unrolled the package with trembling hands.

It was a nice new calendar.

Eugene Field

No gift his genius might have had
Of titles high, in church and state,
Could charm him as the one he bore,
Of children's poet-laureate.

He smilingly pressed aside his bays
And laurel garlands that he won,
And bowed his head for baby hands
To place a daisy wreath upon.

He found his kingdom in the ways,
Of little ones he loved so well,
For them he tuned his lyre and sang.
Sweet simple songs of magic spell.

Ah! greater feat to storm the gates
Of children's pure and cleanly hearts,
Than to subdue a warring world
By stratagems and doubtful arts.

A tribute paid by chanting choirs
And pealing organs rises high;
But soft and clear, somewhere he hears
Through all, a child's low lullaby.

Slightly Mixed

A certain Houston racing man was married some months ago. He also is the proud possessor of a fine two-year-old filly that has made five and a half furlongs in 1:09 and he expects her to do better at the next races. He has named the filly after his wife and both of them are dear to his heart. A Post man who ran across him yesterday found him quite willing to talk.

"Yes," he said, "I am the happiest man in Texas. Bessie and I are keeping house now and getting quite well settled down. That filly of mine is going to do wonders yet. Bessie takes as much interest in her as I do. You know I have named her for my wife. She is a thoroughbred. I tell you it's fine to see her trotting around at home."

"Who, the filly?"

"No, my wife. She's going to bet twelve dozen pairs of kid gloves on Bessie next time she goes in. I have but one objection to her. She goes with her head on one side and is cross-legged, and tears off her shoes.

"Your w-w-wife?"

"No, what's the matter with you? The filly. It pleases me very much to have my friends inquire about Bessie. She is getting to be quite a favorite. I had hard work to get her, too. She trots double without a break."

"The filly, you mean?"

"No, my wife. I took Bessie out driving with the filly yesterday. Bessie's a daisy. She's a little high in one shoulder, and a trifle stiff in one leg, but her wind is all right. What do you think of her back?"

"Really, I—I—I never had the pleasure of meeting your wife, but I have no doubt—"

"What are you talking about? I mean the filly. The races come off just on the anniversary of our marriage. The races are going to be a big thing. You know we have been married just a year. I expect Bessie to do wonders. There's a newcomer going to be here, that we are looking for with much interest. You must really come out and see our first event."

"I—I—I really, it would be indelicate—you must really excuse me. I never saw anything of the kind. I—I—"

"Oh, there's nothing wrong about horse racing. It's fine sport. So long now. I've got to go and take Bessie out and sweat her a little."

Knew What Was Needed

A gentleman from Ohio, who has come South on a hunting trip, arrived in Houston, rather late one night last week, and on his way to a hotel stopped in a certain saloon to get a drink. A colored man was behind the bar temporarily and served him with what he wanted. The gentleman had his shotgun in its case, and he laid it upon the bar while waiting.

"Is there any game about here?" he asked, after paying for his drink.

"I guess dey is, boss," said the colored man, looking doubtfully at the gun on the counter, "but you jest wait a minute, boss, till I fixes you up in better shape."

He opened a drawer and handed the gentleman a six-shooter.

"You take dis, Boss," he said. "Dat dar gun ob yourn am too long fur you to get quick action in de game what we hab here. Now you jest go up dem steps and knock free times on de doah to your left."

Some Ancient News Notes

It will be remembered that a short while ago, some very ancient documents and records were discovered in an old monastery on Mt. Sinai, where they have been kept filed away by the monks among their dusty archives. Some of them antedate the oldest writings previously known by one hundred years. The finders claim that among them are the original Scripture traced in Syriac language, and that they differ in many material ways from the translation in use. We have procured some advance sheets from the discoverers and in a few fragments given below our readers will perceive that human nature was pretty much the same a thousand years ago. It is evident from the palimpsests in our possession that newspapers were not entirely unknown even at that early date. We give some random translations from the original manuscripts:

"Commodore Noah, one of our oldest citizens, predicts a big rain soon. The commodore is building an up-to-date houseboat and expects to spend about six weeks afloat with his family and his private menagerie."

"Colonel Goliath of Gath, and the new middleweight, Mr. David, are at their old tricks again blowing about the championship. Mr. David has one hand in a sling, but says he will be all right when the affair is pulled off. A little more fighting and less talking would please the readers of the Daily Cymbal."

"Ladies, get one of those new fig leaves at the Eden Bazaar before the style is dropped."

"The exposition at Shinar is going to be a grand success. Work on the New Woman's Building called the Tower of Babel has been stopped on account of a misunderstanding. The lady managers have been holding meetings in the Tower for some time."

"See Professor Daniel and his performing lions next Sunday."

"Colonel Job, who has been suffering from quite a siege of boils at his residence on Avenue C, was arrested yesterday for cussing and disturbing the neighborhood. The colonel has generally a very equable temper, but completely lost his balance on finding that Mrs. Job had put a large quantity of starch in his only night robe."

"About 1,500 extra deputy clerks were put on by the county clerk yesterday to assist in getting out summonses for witnesses in the divorce case recently brought by Judge Solomon against the last batch of his wives."

A Sure Method

The editor sat in his palatially furnished sanctum bending over a mass of manuscripts, resting his beetling brow upon his hand. It wanted but one hour of the time of going to press and there was that editorial on the Venezuelan question to write. A pale, intellectual youth approached him with a rolled manuscript tied with a pink ribbon.

"It is a little thing," said the youth, "that I dashed off in an idle moment."

The editor unrolled the poem and glanced down the long row of verses. He then drew from his pocket a $20 bill and held it toward the poet. A heavy thud was heard, and at the tinkle of an electric bell the editor's minions entered and carried the lifeless form of the poet away.

"That's three today," muttered the great editor as he returned the bill to his pocket. "It works better than a gun or a club and the coroner always brings in a verdict of heart failure."

Endnotes

The methods of the Rev. Sam Jones, who was the Billy Sunday of his time, were frequently the subject of O. Henry's satire. ↩

Milton Keynes UK
Ingram Content Group UK Ltd.
UKHW021557260524
443160UK00005B/338

9 789361 475801